Elaine Moore Moffat

BLUE RIBBON HORSEWOMAN

The complete life story of a
champion rider who learned to cope with life
by learning to deal with horses

by Grace Walker

A RUTLEDGE BOOK
THOMAS NELSON & SONS
London · New York · Toronto

This is an Authorized Biography

PHOTO CREDITS

All photos by Walter Vecchio except the following:
Budd, Pages 14, 51, 64, 68
Freudy Photos, Pages 4, 28, 55 — Scott, Page 62
Tarrance Photographs, Pages 12, 36, 86

CONTENTS

Elaine Moore Moffat, blue ribbon winner and champion horsewoman

Chapter One

END
OF A
DREAM

The farmhouse was quiet in the cold sunlight of a February afternoon. It was so quiet that Elaine Moffat, waiting in her living room, could hear the ticking of the kitchen clock.

Tick, tick, tick, tick ... and with every tick Elaine heard the words "Swamp fever—swamp fever ..."

She pressed her hands over her ears, as if by shutting out the sound of that clock she could shut out this terrible day. She shuddered as the crack of a rifle rang out in the cold air, followed by the whinnying scream of a dying horse.

In the lower pasture of their farm, her husband, John, was destroying the horses that they and their young children had loved, trained, ridden, and cared for. It was the destruction of a dream that had become reality only after years of brutally hard work.

Six months ago a telephone call had come in the middle of the night. John had picked up the phone to hear a neighbor's voice shouting, "One of your horses is tearing up my vegetable garden! Get down here fast!"

"Is it Roulette?" Elaine had asked anxiously as John jumped out of bed and started to dress. "Oh, John, what's the matter with him?"

"I don't know, but I've got to get down there." John pulled on a sweater. "He could hardly stand up this morning. How'd he get out of his stall, much less jump a four-foot fence?" He stopped at the door to say, "Don't worry, now—I'll be back soon."

Don't worry! For days the Moffats had done little except worry about Roulette. He was the first horse John had ever owned, a favorite not only with the family but with most of the better horsemen who rode out of the Moffat stables. The week before he had suddenly developed alarming symptoms. Strange bumps had appeared all over his glossy hide, and his eyes had swollen shut. A local veterinarian had given him a shot that seemed to have some effect, but it had been clear that Roulette was a sick horse.

But—how sick? And with what? Elaine knew she would sleep no more that night. Getting up, she pulled on a robe and huddled up on the window seat, ears alert for the clip-clop of Roulette's hoofs along the road that ran past the farmhouse. But there was only silence, and a growing fear . . and then after a long time the opening and closing of the back door, and John's footsteps on the stairs.

Standing in the doorway of the moonlit room, he said, "I had to put him down, Elaine. I don't know what it was. In all my years around horses I've never seen anything like it—it was like watching a mad dog! He kept staggering around in circles. It was risking your life just to go near him. Finally I got a rope around his neck and Jimmy went into the house and got his gun—" John sat down heavily on the side of the bed. "I shot him, Elaine. I had to."

"Oh, no!" Elaine cried. "How awful! But what *was* it?"

John had shaken his head. "That's just it. We can't have him die that way without knowing why. I think we ought to take him to the clinic at Cornell University and have an autopsy."

So it had begun. And now, six months later, it was ending—with those rifle shots.

The day after Roulette's death, Roany, the workhorse, had dropped dead. And still Cornell University could not be positive about what was the matter.

"If it's what we think it is," one of their vets told John over the phone, "it's bad. But we can't be sure unless we can inject the blood of a sick, living horse into a young, healthy horse who has never been exposed to any illness."

All that was left of their dream was the farm itself. The horses they had worked so hard to train had been destroyed

By the end of the week, Milkshake, beloved of all the children who rode at the Moffats' stable, was ill. Shipped to Cornell, Milkshake died within hours. But he had lived long enough for the government veterinarians to take a sample of his blood and inject it into one of their test horses—groups of which are kept at testing centers all over the country.

Two days later a government veterinarian brought the bad news to the Moffats' busy stables. With him came quarantine notices which were tacked to the sides of the white-painted barn. The Moffat stables were out of business. No horse could be brought into, or taken from, the premises. Stunned, Elaine and John learned that Roulette and the others had died of swamp

10

fever—the dreaded, uncontrollable disease that few stables ever survived.

That had been six months before—six months of testing, waiting, praying. Six months of listening for the crack of rifle fire from the lower pasture, for the screams of the doomed horses who sensed what was happening. Elaine and John had loved these horses. They were Western animals who had never known a bit in their mouths or a saddle on their backs until they were painstakingly broken, schooled, and gentled by the Moffats. Their deaths meant ruin for the stable, and heartbreak for the young couple.

For Elaine and John, nothing was left. All the horses were gone, except the thoroughbred mare that had been a gift to Elaine from her mother on her sixteenth birthday. The stalls would be there, empty, to greet the Moffat children, Michael and Pamela, when they came home tomorrow from an overnight visit to a friend.

"Five years of hard work," Elaine thought, "and now we have nothing to show for it but those empty stalls!" A wave of fear washed over her. They'd had such plans—they'd worked so hard, and in one steady direction! What would they do now? Feeling tears near, she got up and began to pace the room. A long time ago Elaine had learned that action—any kind of action—was the best way to keep back the tears when there was no time for them.

Pamela, Elaine and John Moffat's little girl, now eight years old, had learned to love and ride horses at the Moffat farm

Restlessly, she fingered the gleaming silver trophies scattered about the room, trophies she had begun to collect when she was eight years old. She picked up the big silver bowl on which was engraved: *National Horsemanship Champion . . . The Alfred B. Maclay Memorial Trophy.* How scared she had been that night, her first night at Madison Square Garden! Holding the bowl, Elaine felt her present fear merge into the memory of the fear of that night so many years ago, when she had been sure that the beginning or the end of the world hinged on what happened.

"I lived through that," she reminded herself. "I lived through a hundred other times when I was frightened. I must have learned something from all of that!"

The threat of tears was gone. If little Elaine Moore hadn't died of fear, grown-up Elaine Moore Moffat wasn't going to die of it either. It was true she had never been through anything so close to complete disaster before—but hadn't all those other crises seemed bad at the time?

Moving among the pictures of herself as a thin child, pictures at shows, at school, she came to one that took her back to her very first horse show at Sands Point, Long Island. She hadn't been scared that day—far from it! The pretty, arrogant little eight-year-old in that picture had been far too cocksure of herself to be scared of anything. Perhaps that was why the memory came back so vividly. The lesson she had learned that day had been so sharp!

"Maybe you've never taken orders before!" She could almost hear again the harsh, cold voice of Gordon Wright, her riding instructor. "But anyone who rides with me takes orders—and you'll take them now!"

The farmhouse living room, the bleak day outside faded away. Elaine was back in the past, back to that day when she had taken a ribbon and ground it into the dirt with the heel of her boot, while the other kids looked on, wide-eyed and horrified.

Elaine took her first ribbon when she was eight and kept on winning

Chapter Two

REBEL
ON
HORSEBACK

"Elaine—do me a favor?" Myles Fletcher spoke softly so that his father, up front in the driver's seat, would be unable to hear over the sound of the car. Elaine Moore sat back and gave her friend a suspicious look. It was nerve-racking enough to be eight years old and on your way to ride in your very first horse show. But Myles was now going to give her "advice for her own good!"

Myles flushed under her look. "Just this once, Elaine, try to keep your mouth shut and—well, do what Mr. Wright says? You know. Take orders. Like the rest of us."

Elaine flushed, too, with annoyance. "You're talking as if I were a baby. I've been riding with Gordon Wright long enough to know what to do."

"Yes, but you don't always do it," Myles said.

"Like last week when you got up on Mad Hen right after he told you to take one of the other horses—anyway, all I'm saying is, Sands Point is your first show and it's important for all the Secor Farms kids to look good and ride well."

Elaine looked at him coldly. "Mad Hen is *my* horse, isn't she? And don't worry about me, I'll ride well. You worry about yourself!" In her anger she had raised her voice. Myles's father, glancing at her in the mirror, said, "Now, kids, you should be calming each other down instead of riling each other up!"

Speaking together, Elaine and Myles said, "I'm sorry," and then burst out laughing. "I guess I am jumpy," Elaine admitted to Myles. "After all, you're two years older and you've been to lots of horse shows. I bet the morning of your first one you were ready to jump down everybody's throat!"

Mr. Fletcher laughed, and Myles said, "I sure was. And I didn't have anything like those new breeches of yours to build me up, either. That's a great-looking get-up, Small Change."

Small Change was an endearing nickname hung on her by the older kids in the horse-show group, as Elaine was the littlest rider going over the biggest fences on the circuit.

Elaine smiled, patting the brand-new canary yellow breeches. She had been up before seven, unable to wait another minute before putting them on. She and Myles rode at Secor Farms Riding Stables every chance there was: all day Saturday, many Sundays, almost every afternoon after school for whatever hours of daylight were left. But their everyday riding clothes took plenty of abuse and were nothing like the elegant outfit her mother had bought for this very special event. First had come the specially tailored breeches. Next, the tall black boots. Then a white shirt, and the white stock which she had painstakingly learned how to "butterfly." Finally, the glen plaid jacket and the black velvet hunt cap, with its elastic band to keep it from flying off her head over jumps.

Picking up her tan gloves and short hunting crop, she had gone downstairs to try to swallow some breakfast. But by eight sharp when Mr. Fletcher finally hooted from the driveway she had been wandering around the hall for ten minutes, too keyed up to sit down.

Myles's blue eyes crinkled at her. "I hope you don't break up any jumps by falling off in those new breeches."

"I won't fall off today," Elaine said confidently. "After my last round on Mad Hen, Mr. Wright schooled her himself. I'll be fine. But gosh," she burst out, "I wish I were allowed to school my own horse— the way you do."

"You will be, when you're as old as I am," Myles said. Elaine grinned at the slim boy beside her—much

Spoiled and headstrong, Elaine Moore had to learn that she herself must be schooled and gentled just as horses are

heavier than her fifty pounds, to be sure, and much taller than she. "You're lucky you're not fat," she said. "Mr. Wright says it's hard to have a good seat on a horse if you have a round leg. Like that girl Betsy— Mr. Wright says she'll never be a good rider until she goes on a diet."

Mr. Fletcher let out a deep sigh. "You and Myles," he said. "Horses, horses, horses. Don't you ever think of anything else?"

"Sure," Myles said. "Lessons, and new boots, and the last time Mr. Wright bawled us out." And he and Elaine laughed, not because what he said was funny, but because they were on their way to do what they both loved more than anything else in the world—ride a horse over jumps.

For one fleeting moment, as Mr. Fletcher joined in their laughter, Elaine wished that her mother could have come along too and shared the fun. Then she put the thought aside. She already knew that a person couldn't have everything. It was because her mother was always so busy writing stories, and meeting deadlines, that there was enough money for beautiful riding clothes and private lessons—and maybe, soon, for a really top show horse all her own, when Gordon Wright said she was ready for it. And if she could do well today, and earn her ribbon, her mother would be just as happy to have her come home and tell about it as if she'd been there herself.

"Mr. Wright said we were to go straight to our van and wait for him," Myles said, breaking into her thoughts. "Then we each can have a schooling session. I'll be riding On Guard in three open classes, so we'll probably have to rap him with a bamboo stick. I guess Mr. Wright will put one of his top riders up on him for that. I wish he'd let me do it. I wouldn't mind falling off if I could ride my own horse for the schooling!"

"I just can't understand why you all let Mr. Wright order you around like that," Elaine said impatiently. "I mean, On Guard is *your* horse! If you want to school him I don't see what Mr. Wright has to do with it. Do you, Mr. Fletcher?"

"Don't get me into this," Mr. Fletcher said. "If Myles wants to talk to Mr. Wright about it, it's all right with me. But when you've picked a teacher because he knows his business, I think you ought to go along with his rules—or get another teacher."

"That's just what I would do if Mr. Wright ever bawled me out the way he does some of the older riders," Elaine said defiantly. "I'd go down and ride with Brooks Jenkins at Silver Birch. Do you know one day Mr. Wright had Mrs. Dean in *tears?* I'd like to see him make *me* cry!"

Myles squirmed. "There you go again. Look, Elaine, Mr. Wright's your instructor. That means he knows more than you do, right? You're there to learn, and if you want to learn from him you've got to do it his way. You know perfectly well that if you get him down on you you won't be the one who switches to Silver Birch—Mr. Wright'll send you away himself!"

Elaine stared at the green countryside going by. It was true enough that many kids had been "fired" from Secor Farms Riding Stables because Mr. Wright didn't think they were serious enough about their riding. Gordon Wright was only interested in making champions. But he would never fire her. Her mother would find a way to get her out of this, as she always had before. Besides, she was too good a rider. One day she was going to be a champion. And Gordon Wright knew it!

"There's the sign!" Elaine said, sitting forward eagerly. Nailed to a tree was a poster that announced: *Sands Point Horse Show — On the grounds of the Sands Point Riding and Hunt Club — Next Right.*

The car turned and slowed. Elaine was nervous again. Had the groom remembered to braid Mad Hen's mane and tail? What would the jumps be like? Who'd be the judge?

"There's our van," Myles said, as the car bumped over the grassy field to the ringside parking space. "And there's Mr. Wright and the others. See you later, Dad!"

"Thanks for the ride," Elaine added. Almost before the car stopped she and Myles tumbled out to run across the wet grass to the little group of which Gordon Wright was the center.

"Okay, Elaine," Mr. Wright greeted her. "Go get Mad Hen and walk her—I said *walk* her—over the outside course. In case I decide to let you go into a hunter class."

Elaine stared at him. "But I'm entered in *four* hunter classes. Don't you remember?"

"I remember perfectly," Mr. Wright said. "But with all the rain we had last night, the going out there is pretty slippery. If the sun comes out to dry it up, fine. If not, you'll just stick to the horsemanship-over-jumps classes and the Maclay, in the ring."

Elaine opened her mouth to protest, caught Myles's warning look, and said instead, "Yes, Mr. Wright." Going slowly to the back of the van, she found Mad Hen and polished her until the chestnut coat shone.

Bill, the groom, gave her a leg up into the saddle. As she headed toward the outside course, the more experienced riders were taking their mounts over practice jumps in the ring. She saw Langston Wilder climb aboard On Guard to take him over a low fence. Just as he got on top of the fence, Mr. Wright struck the horse over the knees with a light bamboo pole. It didn't hurt, but the cracking sound, and the fact that he could not see the pole, startled the horse. Next time he was almost two feet above the jump. After a few more raps, Myles got on On Guard himself and rode him over the fence without a "poling."

As Elaine had learned during her lessons with Gordon Wright, there are two kinds of jumping horses—open jumpers and hunters. On Guard was an open jumper; Mad Hen was a hunter. A hunter is never "poled," as On Guard had been, because a hunter should not jump too high. In the hunt field, if a hunter "stands back" and "sails" over fences, it becomes exhausted in a very short time.

A hunt, for which a hunter is bred, trained, and

raised, may start at four o'clock in the morning and not end before three that afternoon. It was easy to see why a habit of high jumping would, as Mr. Wright explained, take too much out of a hunter. That was why On Guard had to be "poled" to teach him to take his fences high, while Mad Hen had only to walk the course and get used to the sights and sounds of the horse show.

As the hot, muggy day wore on, the clouds grew heavier, obscuring the sun. The grass on the outside course was well trampled down now and slippery as glass. "Just the same," Elaine told herself, "everyone knows what a great hunter Mad Hen is. Mr. Wright knows that she's even carried Mother out in the hunt field—and she's the most nervous rider in the world! He just can't be mean enough to keep me out of those hunter classes—not on Mad Hen!"

Still, Elaine knew that was just what Mr. Wright would do if he thought the course was too slippery. And there was the next hunter class lining up! It was a "Ladies' Hunter" class—and surely Mad Hen was made to order for a ladies' hunter class! "I'm going to do it!" Elaine thought, and rode quickly over to the line-up.

Mr. Wright was standing over by the ring as Elaine leaned forward and gave her number to the steward in charge of the outside course. Mr. Trowbridge, the announcer, called out, "Next over the

On Mad Hen, at Sands Point, Elaine won her first trophy.
Mad Hen carried her to many victories in her riding career

outside course, number eighteen, Miss Elaine Moore on Mad Hen."

By then she was already making her little circle, easing Mad Hen into a canter, then smoothly, calmly, heading her toward the first fence—a very low brush. As Mad Hen went over it, the last of Elaine's nervousness vanished. This was *fun,* and Mad Hen had never gone better in her life, bending as she made her turn at the far end of the course, leaning lightly into the bit without pulling as they cleared the in-and-out, the chicken coop, the stone wall, then coming to a smooth, perfect stop at the far side of the fence.

Mr. Wright was still at the ringside. Perhaps he hadn't heard her name being called out. And even if he had—so what? Her own mother had given her permission to enter the hunter class! Who was Gordon Wright to tell her she couldn't?

The judges were in a huddle in the center of the field. The card showing the winning numbers was given to a steward, who carried it to Mr. Trowbridge.

"We now have the results of the Ladies' Hunter Class for the Donovan Memorial Trophy," Mr. Trowbridge announced. "First place, a brand-new rider, Miss Elaine Moore of New Rochelle, New York, riding Mrs. Don Moore's horse, Mad Hen."

Elaine couldn't believe her good luck. Of course, Mad Hen was a made-to-order ladies' hunter. And Mr. Wright had given the mare her final schooling himself the night before—that made a difference. Just the same, it was terrific!

As she trotted back toward the van, all kinds of people came up to congratulate her—people she didn't know but who suddenly knew her, because she was a winner.

Bill, the groom, said, "Nice going, Elaine," as he handed her the blue ribbon from Mad Hen's bridle. "That was a big class you won—and you deserved it. Mr. Wright'll be proud of you!"

But none of the kids from Secor Farms came near her. Elaine's heart began to beat in a jumpy, nervous way. Gordon Wright was still at the ringside, watching Myles get a fourth in the amateurs' open jumper class. Slowly, clutching the small replica of the Donovan Trophy, which had to be won three times by the same rider for permanent possession, Elaine went toward the ring.

The last classes, to decide the championships in the different divisions, were about to be run off. Myles came out of the ring with his ribbon and turned his horse over to one of the grooms. He joined the group of young riders lounging against the rail near Mr. Wright. Elaine went up to Myles and said to him, rather uncertainly, "Hi."

None of the kids looked at her. Not even Myles. But Mr. Wright turned around and gave her a long, steady stare. "Elaine, I think I told you not to enter the hunter class unless I okayed it—or was I dreaming?"

"No, Mr. Wright—I mean you did tell me." Elaine gave him a tentative smile. "But it wasn't that slippery—and Mad Hen's been going so well all day, I knew she'd take care of me. And I did win, Mr. Wright! I won the whole class!" The words died on her lips.

Mr. Wright said quietly, "I know you're not used to taking orders. I hoped you were learning. When I tell my kids to do something, they do it. And when I tell them not to do something, they don't. So go put the ribbon and the trophy in the car—and tomorrow I'll talk to your mother about shipping Mad Hen down to Silver Birch or any other place you want to send her. You won't be riding with me any more."

He nodded curtly and walked off. Blazing with humiliation, Elaine threw down the ribbon and stamped it into the dirt with her boot. "Who needs to? There are plenty of other places!" she cried out.

But Myles, beside her, was shaking his head. "Darn it all, Elaine," he said miserably, "I told you it would be like this! Now we can't ride together any more."

Elaine found herself alone with Myles as the other kids moved slowly off.

"I know," she said, "they all think I'm just a spoiled brat, don't they?"

Myles's silence was her answer.

Elaine learned to take, in proper form, the most difficult jumps

Chapter Three

TAKING
ORDERS

"It's not fair!" Elaine stormed. "It's just not fair! I won the class, didn't I? And Mad Hen is my horse. And you *said* I could ride in a class over the outside course. So why do I have to take orders from Mr. Wright?"

The small, dark-haired woman seated on the sofa twisted her fingers in her lap, trying to decide what to say to her daughter.

"I'll take Elaine on," Gorden Wright had said, "because she's got talent for riding. Lots of talent. But when I give an order, I expect it to be obeyed. And she's not going to run to you. Because if she does, it won't do her a bit of good."

Isabel Moore knew perfectly well that her daughter was a spoiled girl. But, as she had said to Elaine's stepfather, Don Moore, "She needs some spoiling. For four years I hardly saw her, I was so busy getting an education, becoming a writer. Now she's just a frightened little girl. She doesn't know you well at all. She hardly knows me. She doesn't remember her father—"

Elaine's mother had been only seventeen when Elaine was born. When the going got rough, during the last of the depression days, Elaine's father had, quite simply, vanished.

"We've got to go out of our way to be kind to her, to spoil her a little—" Elaine's mother had said to the gentle, kindly man who had adopted Elaine when he married her mother.

Then there had been the years of chronic bronchitis and endless colds and pneumonia, all calling for still more petting and pampering. When Elaine's younger sister, Pamela, was born, Elaine's mother had felt even more strongly the need to let Elaine know that she was loved and dearly wanted. Now, the little girl who needed spoiling was to learn a lesson.

"Elaine," her mother said finally, "you don't have to take orders from Mr. Wright. No one in this world has to do anything she doesn't want to do—if she's willing to pay the price. And you don't have to ride at Secor Farms."

Her mother placed a reassuring hand on Elaine's shoulder and went on: "Today you won a blue ribbon —and a fight against authority. Tomorrow you and I will drive over to Silver Birch and see whether it was worth it. Now, darling, it's time you went to bed."

"I won't!" Elaine thought, tossing and turning on the big bed in her pink-and-white bedroom. "I won't do what Myles wants me to do, and apologize to Mr. Wright. I won't, I won't . . ."

In the morning, she sat beside her mother in the station wagon. They turned in at the wide, well-cared-for driveway of the Silver Birch Club. The buildings, low and white-painted, slept in the sunlight of the summer morning. Here was none of the feverish activity that was always going on at Secor Farms. For the most part, the members of Silver Birch were older people—Sunday riders, hack riders. And Brooks Jenkins, who came out to meet them, was primarily the trainer of thoroughbred race horses.

"Well," Brooks greeted them cheerfully, "this is a pleasant surprise. Hear you won a big class on Mad Hen out at Sands Point yesterday."

"She did," Elaine's mother said quickly, "but Elaine just had an idea that—well—that maybe she'd like to bring Mad Hen back here."

The expression on Brooks's face changed. After an awkward moment, he said, "Gosh, Elaine, we'd love to have you, but I'm afraid there isn't a single empty stall in the barn."

Elaine and her mother sat in stunned silence. They understood what Brooks was trying to say—he didn't want her back!

For a minute, Brooks studied the child's stubborn face. He knew that children are a lot like horses. It's much harder to straighten out a spoiled horse, or a spoiled child, than it is to keep him going straight in the first place.

"Well, Elaine," he said slowly, "why don't you tell Gordon Wright you're sorry about whatever it was you did, and let it go at that? All your friends are up there. It wouldn't be much fun for you here."

"Thanks, Brooks," Elaine's mother said quickly. "Actually I think she should stick with Gordon Wright."

The car backed out of the driveway and neither Elaine nor her mother spoke for a time.

Elaine's mother was the first to break the silence. "All right," she said, "so Brooks doesn't want to take you back. I know it hurts, but that's the way it is."

"But, mother," Elaine protested, close to tears, "I can't go up there and apologize to Mr. Wright. The other kids will think I have no pride."

Her mother reached over to comfort her. "Darling," she said, "it takes courage to admit you were wrong, and this time you *were* wrong. You acted like a spoiled brat. I've always taught you that the most important thing in life was to win. When I took you up to Gordon Wright, I told him I wanted him to make a champion of you. But everyone who's ever got to the top—in anything—has had to learn one thing: discipline. I had to learn it. Gordon Wright

*Work and more work—like indoor practice at Secor Farms—
was Elaine's rule in learning to become a great horsewoman*

had to. Your horses have to learn it. And so, darling,
will you, if you're ever going to be a champion."

"But you always said that rules are made to be
broken!" Elaine protested.

Her mother ran a finger around the rim of the
steering wheel. "Yes, I know. I said that rules were
made to be broken and that signposts are put up for
people who can't find their way through life alone.
But to break rules just because they're there is pretty
childish."

Suddenly, the landscape blurred before Elaine's
eyes. "I don't understand," she muttered, "it seems to
me that grown-ups are always telling kids to do something and then, when they do it, telling them to do

something else. I thought you'd be so *proud* of me—"

"I am proud of you. But I'll be even more proud if you can see that disobeying an order from your teacher was wrong. Winning the class didn't make it right."

"All right," she told her mother. "Let's go up to Secor and see what Mr. Wright has to say."

When they arrived, Elaine sat in the car while her mother went into the little office. Through the dusty window she could see the two of them talking, Mr. Wright gesturing angrily every now and then with the red appointment book.

She got out of the car as her mother emerged from the office at the side of the low, white stucco buildings. Mr. Wright followed, wearing his usual hunting cap, tall riding boots, and yellow breeches.

"Okay, Elaine," he said. "I'll give you one more chance. Go in and get Princess."

"Princess!" Elaine repeated, and her face fell. Princess was the oldest horse in the stable, and lame in all four legs. She was kept for elderly ladies and very young children. The worst disgrace that could be handed to anyone at Secor was to be told to ride Princess.

"That's right," Gordon Wright said cheerfully. "Tell Bill to tack up Princess, then take her in the little ring beside the stable and put her on a left lead. As soon as you've got her on a left lead, let me know, and I'll give you something else."

Elaine's spirits rose a little. That wasn't so bad. She knew all about getting a horse on a proper lead by moving the horse's hindquarters. It was only when you let a horse "roll" into a lead from his forelegs that he got onto the wrong lead.

A horse must take his proper lead because, Elaine knew, if he doesn't, when going around in a circle, his front legs will cross and he may fall down. When a horse is galloping on a straightaway, the lead does not matter, as a horse will shift automatically from one to another.

To put a horse on a lead, either right or left, Elaine had been taught, the rider sits very still, brings the horse to a walk, and closes his fingers on the line which tightens the rein. This holds the horse's head in place while the rider's legs close on him. With one leg, the horse's hindquarters are moved in toward the fence. Thrown off balance, the horse will automatically rear out with the opposite foreleg— and take his lead. Some horses find this more difficult than others, and for horses that are very old or somewhat lame, as Princess was, it was almost impossible—as Elaine was to find out.

Meanwhile, she was glad she'd swallowed her pride. She had begun to think that Mr. Wright's bark was worse than his bite as she climbed up on the mounting block and got on poor, old, swayback

35

Going after the Maclay is not only a matter of riding. A champion will school, train and care for her own horse

Princess. She led her into the small ring, walked her to get the kinks out of her old legs, let her trot for a while, then settled down to serious business.

Other cars drove up to the stable and parked. Myles, Roger, Sue, Archie—one by one they got out of the cars, waved to their parents and went to get their horses. Elaine watched them line up with Mr. Wright on the outside course. The sun rose higher. She began to perspire. Finally, everyone went off to

Hunter's Lodge for lunch. Elaine stuck it out. Then everyone came back from lunch, got fresh horses, and headed for the outside course again. The sun began to sink. Princess could barely put one leg in front of the other.

And then, miraculously, Princess took her left lead. She broke, took it again, broke, took it again, held it. Exhausted and hungry, Elaine trotted toward the outside course to report her triumph.

"Mr. Wright," Elaine said, "I've got her on a left lead."

The other riders came up to watch.

"That's wonderful, Elaine!" Mr. Wright answered. "Take her around the stone wall."

Holding her breath, Elaine took the mare around the stone wall in a slow, gentle canter. Princess took her left lead and held it as though she had never in her life thought of going any other way.

"Okay," Mr. Wright called out, "that's great. Just great. You know," he told Elaine, with a grin that creased his sun-browned, square-jawed face, "I've had that mare twenty-five years, and that's the first time I've ever seen anyone get her on a left lead. So you see," he turned to tell the boys and girls gathered around him, "there's nothing you can't get a horse to do if you make up your mind. Okay, Elaine, you can take her in now. And I've a brand-new horse for you tomorrow."

As a member of Golden's Bridge Hunt, Elaine could wear the "colors"

Chapter Four

TROUBLE

The white stucco house on Lovell Road was an active place, full of Elaine's friends, the sound of her mother's typewriter, and the joy of watching her baby sister grow. But sometimes it was a lonely place.

Often Elaine asked, "When is Don coming home from the Army?" It would be pleasant to have her quiet, gentle stepfather near, the family complete.

Always Mrs. Moore answered, "Not for a while yet, dear," and her voice would trail away. Once she asked, "How would you feel about our selling the house and moving down to Washington?"

"I don't know," Elaine said. Give up their home? Give up riding, and Secor Farms—especially now, with True Gold to ride? It still seemed more dream than reality that her mother had actually bought True Gold—not just a good hunter, but a real show horse.

But sometimes even True Gold wasn't enough. Sometimes—on weekends, when her friends' fathers were around—Elaine felt a kind of emptiness. She would push the feeling down, turn to Myles for companionship, lose herself in the important business of learning to be a better and better rider.

When Elaine was ten years old, Gordon Wright took her, with Myles and two other riders, up to Golden's Bridge. There she experienced the excitement of her first fox hunt.

Now her obedience and self-discipline made Elaine one of the most welcome members of the hunt. Horse and rider responded instantly to every order—doing, not questioning—while the other young riders were earning frowns from the older members of the hunt for talking, for not being able to hold their horses, for riding up front.

During her second season with the Golden's Bridge Hunt, when she was twelve, Elaine was awarded her "colors." This meant that when she went to a horse show, she could wear the red collar, the brass buttons with GB on them, the yellow vest and patent leather boot tops that mean a rider is a qualified member of a recognized hunt.

On her thirteenth birthday, Elaine asked Gordon Wright, "When are you going to let me ride in the Garden and try to win my Maclay?"

"One of these days," Mr. Wright assured her,

as he drove her and Myles back to Secor Farms. "The day I look up and see you doing everything perfectly on a horse—that's when I'll tell you to get him braided up, because we're going down to Madison Square Garden!"

The Maclay class is open to amateur riders who have not reached their eighteenth birthday. If the rider wins the Maclay class three times in one season he becomes eligible to compete for the Maclay Trophy in the finals at the National Horse Show in Madison Square Garden. It is a memorial trophy, given by Alfred B. Maclay for kindness to animals, but it stands for much more. To win it, a young rider must have good hands—he never jabs a horse in the mouth by being left in the saddle when the horse takes a jump. The rider proves that he has treated his horse well because he responds quietly to the rider's instructions and never becomes excited. It is the supreme test of a young rider's courage and horsemanship, his obedience to the rules.

Elaine had qualified this year with three wins to compete for the trophy. But she knew that Madison Square Garden wasn't just another local horse show. She would be up against tremendous competition, the most polished young riders from all over the country. Until Mr. Wright said she was ready—well, she just had to go on working, and learning, and waiting.

Elaine learned to love and to care for the needs of the horses at Secor Farms—lessons important to her own growing up

Then, one September afternoon, Gordon Wright came over as Elaine was untacking her horse. "Okay, Elaine, I guess we'll let you go to the Garden in November and make a try for your Maclay."

"Gosh, Mr. Wright, do you think I'm ready?"

"You'd better be ready," he told her with a grin. "We'll let you take Power Plant."

Her face fell. Power Plant was a wonderful little horsemanship horse, but he had no flash. She could not imagine him winning in competition with horses for which other kids' parents had paid up to five thousand dollars. She wished that she could ride True Gold—but he was a hunter, the wrong kind of horse for the Maclay.

"I know Mother will rent a really high-class horse for me, Mr. Wright. She told me so, although she won't be able to buy one."

Gordon Wright shook his head. "Your mother's always anxious for you to have the best, Elaine. But tell her to forget it—right now, all you need is to do *your* best."

It was a relief, anyway, not to have to present her mother with still another problem. Though Elaine's days were crammed with her own doings, she couldn't help being aware that the big white house was no longer a happy place. Letters from Don were few and far apart. It was a long time since Elaine had seen her mother come out of the workroom wearing the look that meant her writing had gone well.

Then, one unforgettable morning, Elaine was made more acutely aware of trouble at home. Pam, her young sister, woke up complaining of a painfully swollen ankle.

"You must have twisted it without noticing," Mrs. Moore comforted her. But Elaine did not miss the worried lines between her mother's eyebrows as together they helped Pam down into the car.

Pam's sickness was diagnosed as rheumatic fever. By the time the doctor was certain of it, Elaine had seen enough of his concern, and her mother's, to realize that rheumatic fever was something pretty serious. One afternoon, as the doctor was leaving, Elaine overheard him telling Mrs. Moore that a calm, secure atmosphere would help Pam as much as anything toward full recovery.

"We can't prove it yet," the doctor said, "but rheumatic fever appears to be one of the diseases that are closely linked to emotional disturbance. As far as Pamela is concerned, we can treat and arrest it—so don't worry on that score. But . . ." The doctor's tone grew very serious. "There's nothing worse for children than an atmosphere of uncertainty."

Unseen, Elaine retreated to her room. The doctor's words translated themselves very simply in her mind . . . were Don and her mother thinking of getting a divorce?

Shortly afterward, Pam had to be taken to White Plains Hospital with a fever and more swellings. Elaine realized that, until Pam was out of danger, her mother would have neither time nor strength to give to other problems.

Elaine fought her own fears by putting everything she had into her riding. It was partly to keep herself going, but partly also because she had a fearful suspicion that if she didn't get her Maclay at Madison Square Garden this November she might not have another chance.

The sense of crisis deepened when her mother told Elaine that Don was coming home. Standing on her mother's velvety rug, still in the yellow breeches and black coat she had worn that morning on a hunt, Elaine tried to read from her mother's expression just what this announcement might mean. "For long?"

Mrs. Moore said, "I honestly don't know, darling. But I think—just for a visit. Things need to be talked about . . ." She stood up and put her arm around Elaine's shoulders. "Don't you worry. You concentrate on your Maclay and I'll concentrate on straightening things out, and getting Pam well."

In her own room, Elaine stripped off the hunting jacket and threw herself on the bed. A stepfather was still a father, even if you hadn't seen him for ages. Besides, what about Pamela?

Elaine sat bolt upright, as another nagging fear took hold. What about money? She looked about the pretty room with its wall-to-wall carpeting, its polished mahogany and crisp chintz. Once there had been plenty of money—everything she'd had and known, at least until lately, had cost a lot of money. And the riding, now, cost more than ever. What would it be like if, from now on, she and Pam and their mother didn't have enough money?

Elaine shivered. She couldn't ask her mother for things any more. Whatever she wanted, whatever she needed, she was going to have to get herself!

"I've got to figure out how to keep on riding, no matter what!" Elaine vowed.

With Elaine, the president of the American Horse Show Association

Chapter Five

BIG NIGHT

The National Horse Show at Madison Square Garden that November evening was to Elaine like a scene from the widest-screen movie ever made—high-stepping five-gaited horses, saddle horses with their docked tails and weighted feet, thoroughbred hunters to be judged in conformation classes, working hunters carrying their honorable hunting scars.

There were the judges in their tall hats and white ties and tails. There was the gabble of many foreign languages. There was Otis Trowbridge, who announced all the large horse shows.

Elaine didn't know anyone and yet she knew everyone. The people here were the people who loved horses and riding as much as she — that was the bond among them.

Best of all, this spangled night, Elaine's mother

had come to see the show. Pam had been taken home from the hospital though she would still have to spend long months in bed. If Elaine did win her Maclay, her mother would be there to share the greatest moment of her riding life.

In addition to the Maclay, Elaine would be showing high-priced thoroughbred hunters for other people. Mr. Wright was, Elaine knew, giving her a big chance—and a big responsibility—as a young trainer as well as a young rider. If she won her Maclay, here at the Garden, more owners would be asking her to ride for them. And with her sister seriously ill, with bills piling up, and her mother beginning to talk about selling the horses, Elaine had already recognized that the amount of riding she could do depended on how well she did here at the Garden tonight.

So the thing to concentrate upon now was the Maclay. "Never put your mind on more than one thing at once," she could remember Mr. Wright bellowing at her across the indoor ring. "And never think about the second jump until you've cleared the first. Then the second will take care of itself."

Because the war years had interrupted the running of the Maclay, three years of Maclay winners would compete for the trophy at this show. Nerves were raw, and the narrow aisles before the stalls in the basement of the Garden were a bedlam of noise and confusion.

"Hi, Small Change!" Myles gave her his usual greeting. "How do you feel?"

"Scared," said Elaine. "Myles, I've just got to win my Maclay this year. Everything is so mixed up at home—I don't even know whether I'll be able to go on riding. Mother's talking about selling the horses."

Myles gave her an understanding nod. "Never mind. You can always ride On Guard, you know."

Elaine's smile thanked him, and she was grateful for the comforting pressure of his hand on her shoulder as, together, they made their way through the confusion of grooms, horses, and riders toward their end of the stable. There was Power Plant, sleek and braided, small and quiet by comparison with some of the horses being brought out by the grooms.

"Who-a, horse!" and "Easy, boy!" were spoken softly by the grooms trying to gentle their high-strung charges. Riding masters from stables from New York to California and back again were giving last-minute instructions.

Gordon Wright was nowhere to be found as Elaine led Power Plant toward the ramp that opened onto the huge indoor ring. "Will you be there when I enter the ring?" Elaine had asked him anxiously earlier in the day.

Mr. Wright had shrugged and said, sensibly, "What's the use? If you don't know by now how to give your horse a good ride and do exactly as the judges tell you, anything I say at the last minute isn't going to help. It's like those horse-show mothers hanging over the ring at a show, yelling at their kids until the poor kids don't know whether they're coming or going. You do the same thing down here that you do at home. Nothing different. And don't listen to a lot of horse-show gossip about how the judges want you to ride. You ride exactly as you've been taught to ride."

So now Elaine was here, on Power Plant, looking out at the ring, hung with its flags of many nations. The boxes were filled with men and women in evening clothes or hunting pinks or regular riding attire. The saddle-seat kids were all at one end, watching the hunter riders come on. They wore their tight-fitting dark-blue jodhpurs and jackets, their derbies, their white shirts and dark ties. Saddle-horse riders didn't wear stocks. Stocks were originally meant to be used as a bandage if a rider was injured in the hunt field. The wearing of them was an ancient English custom carried down to the present.

Elaine tried to think of the important things—like what would happen if she didn't win tonight and never had another chance to compete. Then Otis Trowbridge was calling out her number. Without even feeling the movement, she was out in the ring.

Like a tape recording, Gordon Wright's often-heard instructions went with her as Elaine and Power

Plant took jump after jump, until the eight-jump course was cleared. Then Elaine and six other riders were called back into the ring and given special instructions.

"One at a time," the judge said, "I want you to trot down to the stone wall, clear it, pull up at the other side without letting your horse break into a canter."

Well, that was easy. At home, Mr. Wright had his good riders take four-foot fences from a standstill, or clear whole courses with their arms folded behind their backs or on top of their heads.

One by one, the other kids—many of them about to reach their eighteenth birthday, which would make them ineligible to compete again—tried to follow the

A childhood dream comes alive—horse and rider in perfect harmony as they clear an obstacle at Madison Square Garden

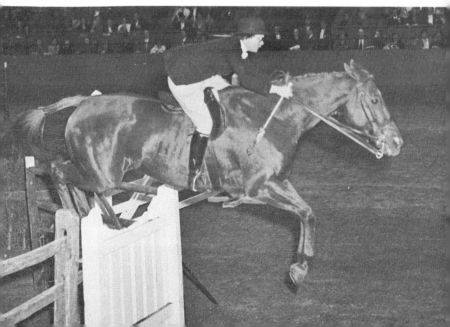

judge's instructions. Almost all of them broke into a canter just before or just after clearing the wall. Elaine felt she practically had the class won as she walked Power Plant halfway back to the other end of the ring, put him into a collected trot.

Just as she approached the fence, a flashlight bulb exploded in the first row of boxes. Some celebrity had had her picture taken. Power Plant ducked away from the noise and sudden exploding light, broke pace—and cleared the fence from a canter!

"It's not fair!" Elaine wanted to burst out as she left the ring, knowing that picture had cost her the first Maclay run-off. But she knew better than to complain to Gordon Wright. His young riders were taught to enter the ring, complete the course, and leave the ring without commenting on the round, the judge, or the class. If they won, the trophy was put instantly out of sight. If they lost, they took it with good grace.

There would be another round, another chance. Wait for that, do better next time. But when Elaine got back to the stables to wait for the next round, she found her mother there. Tense and agitated, she was saying to Gordon Wright, "You've just got to give Elaine another horse! Now that the judges have seen Power Plant being disobedient, they're apt to decide he's not well schooled. Lots of people have offered her top horses. Please, Gordon."

Gordon Wright stood, hands on hips, watching

the flushed, agitated face of the woman before him. "My, my," he said with a shake of the head, "I managed to teach Elaine something about sportsmanship, but it looks as if I should have been teaching you instead! From the time that kid won her first blue ribbon, I've been trying to drum it into her head that *I don't care* whether my kids win or not—but if they *do* win, they've got to win the right way, doing the right thing. And trying to blame her horse for losing a class is about as miserable a thing as a kid can do."

Even as he finished, another young rider, crying bitterly, shoved her horse's reins at her trainer. "You hold him, Joe. I'll teach him to run out on a fence with me!" And, standing close to her horse so he couldn't kick her, she brought her hunting crop down across his shoulders.

"That's what I mean," Gordon Wright said. And to Elaine, "You'll just go right back for the next round and, if necessary for the third round. You'll keep right on doing what you've been taught to do. And if you lose, you'll take it."

When her mother and Gordon Wright moved away, the other kids came piling down the narrow, crowded aisle of the stable. Almost as one, they burst out, "Gosh, Elaine, what a rotten break! But at least Mr. Wright's not going to make you go back on Power Plant, is he?"

"Now that the judges have seen him shy," one

of them told her, "they'll never pin him in a million years."

"*Obedience of horse and rider,*" somebody else quoted. "Man, Power Plant should have read the Maclay rules—he practically exploded down there with that flashbulb!"

As she listened to the voices, mingled with the shouts of the grooms, the whinnying of horses, the sobs and even hysteria of some of the other young riders, Elaine wanted to put her hands to her ears. Instead, she heard again Gordon Wright's words: "No matter what you're up against, you stick to your guns. When you start something, finish it."

"Will the riders for the third running of the Maclay Class—horsemanship over jumps—please bring their horses to the in-gate," intoned the deep, quiet voice of Otis Trowbridge over the loud speaker.

Elaine set her shoulders, tightened her lips, picked up her reins and turned Power Plant back toward the in-gate. Darn it all, Power Plant *was* a good horse, a perfect horsemanship horse, and she would prove it— to the judges, the other kids, everyone! All she had to do, she reminded herself, was to ride her horse.

And ride him she did! There was a good, warm feeling in the pit of Elaine's stomach as she took the last of those eight fences, for she knew that she had cleared the course without a fault. But she'd done that before, she reminded herself . . . don't think about that. Just concentrate on what the judge was saying.

Elaine and six others were chosen to perform again for the judge so that he might choose the winner from among them. As the seven lined up their horses, Elaine could almost hear Gordon Wright saying, "Do your best—that's all anyone can ask of you."

As she went over the fences on a figure-8 course—crossing from side to side of the ring instead of going straight—as the judge required, a sudden sense of great well-being flooded Elaine. She was doing beautifully. Power Plant was doing beautifully. Even if something should happen again, like that flashbulb accident, and she should lose, she knew she was doing her best—and that was all anyone could ask.

Elaine Moore and Power Plant practicing for the Maclay— a combination that won the Madison Square Garden competition

Lined up again, waiting, Elaine tried to read the
judge's face, but could learn nothing from it. She
didn't know she was holding her breath until she
heard herself let it out in a great, profound sigh, when
she heard Otis Trowbridge's voice, "First and champion, Miss Elaine Moore!"

"I made it!" she thought. And then, stroking
Power Plant's neck, *"We* made it—we *made* it!"

For a while there was delirious confusion as Elaine
accepted the huge silver bowl that is the Maclay trophy
from Mr. Van Sinderen, president of the American
Horse Show Association, and as photographers took
pictures of her with the trophy.

Her mother and Myles were both waiting for her,
with Gordon Wright behind them, when she came
through the out-gate. They both hugged her. "Great
going, Small Change," Myles said proudly. "Gordon
was right, as usual," her mother put in. And Gordon
Wright himself, looking as proud as if he had won
the trophy, agreed, grinning, "Of course—I'm always
right when it comes to riding!"

Her mother hugged her again. "Darling, I'm so
proud of you I don't know what to do. I'll tell you
what—let's call home and make sure Pamela's all right,
and then maybe we can all go out and celebrate."

The famous restaurant they went to was full of
horse-show people and horse-show talk that night, buzz-
ing with laughter and excited second-guessing about

what had gone on at the Garden. With Gordon Wright smiling approval, her mother so proudly happy, Myles looking at her as if she were the greatest invention since the wheel, Elaine knew she was spinning in one of her life's high moments.

They had been there only a few minutes when one of the older girls whom she knew slightly stopped by Elaine's chair. "Wasn't it marvelous?" the girl asked. And then, with unmistakable meaning, "Isn't it a shame that your father couldn't be here!" With a little laugh, she was gone.

Elaine put down her glass and held her hands tightly in her lap until they were steady again. With a rush of anger, she thought, "How *dared* she! What business is it of hers! Her parents are divorced—what right has she to criticize mine?"

Then the anger ebbed, and she started to see the funny side. That girl hadn't won a single award all night—and not having been trained by Gordon Wright, she had to take out her poor-loser anger on someone!

Meeting her mother's eyes, Elaine grinned. She'd made her mother happy tonight—and she'd given Gordon Wright the pride and satisfaction of knowing that the effort he'd put into her training hadn't been wasted. With luck . . . with what she was learning about self-control, about obeying the rules and not depending on others for what she wanted . . . well, maybe she could go on to do even better.

Elaine's riding improved each year—now form like this was simple

Chapter Six

A WARY
FRIENDSHIP

"You say *two years,* and it doesn't seem like a very long time," Elaine thought. "But look what can happen in just two years!"

For Elaine, two years had meant the world she had known turned upside down and inside out. At the end of that time, nothing familiar was left but her love for horses, her friendship with Myles, and a close-knit life with her sister Pam and her mother.

Those two years saw Elaine grow from a tall string-bean of a teen-ager to a composed and lovely young woman. They saw her take fantastic losses in her stride because she had learned, by then, that life is a lot like riding—the more you talk about being afraid, the more afraid you get. So she didn't talk about it. Not when she and her mother and sister left for Arizona so that Pamela could get better in the dry, hot desert air. Not even when her mother finally told the girls that the divorce was going through.

Elaine cried about that. She knew Pam cried, too. But there was no point in talking about it because they both knew that the definite act would be better than the uncertainty.

Arizona might have been made to order for a girl who passionately loved horses and needed to be completely occupied. There had been burning sun and sand and desert, round-ups on a real working ranch, cowboys singing beside the fire at night while the stars looked down. There had been mastering western-style riding and being asked by the owner of the ranch to help the men "top off" the dude string—get the horses quiet enough so the guests could ride them along the mountain trails.

Pamela was getting well, gaining weight. Mrs. Moore, away from the reminders of the old way of life, was writing again. A novel had been sold to a top magazine. This meant that Elaine could have the colt her mother had promised her for her sixteenth birthday.

When the doctors said it would be safe to take Pamela back East, Mrs. Moore and the girls made plans together. It would be that way from now on, Elaine knew—the three of them sharing ideas, more like sisters than mother and children.

They arranged that Elaine would go on back to

New Rochelle and help with all the details of selling the big house, while Mrs. Moore took Pamela with her to Las Vegas for the divorce. Elaine felt she was perfectly capable of starting to take a real place in the adult world.

But she no longer felt quite so grown-up when she got back to New Rochelle. She was barely off the plane before she heard from half a dozen people that Myles had been seeing a lot of a new girl named Marian Saunders.

She borrowed a car to drive to the stable—knowing it was the quickest way of running into Myles. He was there, all right. And the minute she saw him, Elaine knew everything she'd heard was true. He looked so uneasy she almost felt sorry for him. He greeted Elaine with a friendly hug, but he wasn't the old Myles—not even when he said how glad he was Pamela was better.

Elaine braced herself. "Mother's gone to Las Vegas to get a divorce."

Myles colored. "I'm sorry," he said. Then, with a quick change of subject, "Mr. Wright just got back from a big hunt meet out in Ohio. Did you know he has your horse for you? A beautiful little two-year-old filly—name's Mint Leaf. Come on!" He tugged her along in the old, easy way.

Halfway down the stable stood one of the most sensational-looking girls Elaine had ever laid eyes on. Her smooth golden hair fell just the way hair is sup-

Going to Scarsdale High, Elaine divided her life between school and stable, with riding of first importance to her

posed to; her skin was honey-colored, and her enormous eyes blazed like sapphires under firm, surprisingly dark brows. Her small, slim body was perfectly turned out in faultless riding clothes.

There was a tiny pause. Then the girl said, "You must be the great rider I've heard so much about. You must be Elaine Moore."

"And you're the great beauty *I've* heard so much about," returned Elaine, pleased that her voice was steady and light. "You're Marian Saunders."

62

The girl gave her a quick, uncertain look, not sure whether she was being complimented or made fun of. Then she grinned, thrust out a hand, and said to Elaine, "Well, if even half of it's true, I guess we can afford to be friends."

Myles said, relief in his voice, "I knew you two would like each other. Marian's a terrific rider," he went on to Elaine, "but, of course, not in your class."

"No," Marian admitted ruefully, "I'm not up to schooling green horses. That takes *nerve.*"

"What doesn't?" Elaine said lightly. She moved along, anxious to get a look at Mint Leaf. The little filly was beautifully fronted, light in the hindquarters, with a fine, small, well-shaped head and good eyes. "If her hindquarter ever grows up to her forehand," Elaine decided, "she ought to be eligible for conformation classes. But even if she isn't, maybe I'll be able to breed her some day. Wouldn't that be fun—to breed your very own mare and raise your very own colt?"

"Sounds terrific," Marian Saunders said. "Now how about all of us going down to Hunter's Lodge for lunch to celebrate your return from Arizona?"

A strange kind of friendship, based on mutual respect, sprang up between the two girls. But, Elaine was to think later, she ought to have known better. How could two attractive girls possibly like one another when they both liked the same boy—who liked both of them!

Famous equestrian Gordon Wright taught Elaine horsemanship rules

Chapter Seven

DISASTER --AND WORSE

The little house Elaine's mother bought in White Plains looked for all the world—as everyone said, admiringly—like a doll's house. It was white clapboard with dark-blue shutters and a smooth stretch of lawn that rolled down to a quiet, tree-lined street. There was also a dog now, a dachshund, which Gordon Wright had given Pamela as a birthday gift.

The girls had chosen their own furnishings— Elaine a pink-and-white room with shelves for horse-show trophies, Pamela a scheme of pale yellow and dark blue. Their mother's room was a combination workroom and bedroom, all in tweeds.

But for all the pretty furnishings and the big, pine-paneled playroom, the house was just a house. Not, as the place on Lovell Road had been, a home. None of them seemed able to get used to it, to feel at ease.

Elaine was now going to Scarsdale High School. Her life was school and the stable—and school was something to be lived through until it was time to go to the stable. She was longeing Mint Leaf now, schooling other horses, and working in the stable on weekends to earn money for the private lessons she could no longer ask her mother to pay for.

Longeing a horse was one of the latest things Elaine had learned. Only a very good horsewoman can longe a horse, and she was proud of the accomplishment. "If a horse is young and mean," Gordon Wright told her, "he might come at you and try to rear up—and bring his front feet down on you. Unless you know how to use the longeing whip, the horse can't be kept far enough away and be forced to keep the gait you want him in.

"You see," he went on, "a young horse doesn't know how to 'take' a bit. A bit will not stop a horse unless he will 'take' it—lean his weight against it. Also, a young horse 'scrambles'—goes from a trot to a canter and back again. The trainer with a young horse on a longe line, with a long longe whip, keeps the horse moving as the trainer wants."

Elaine learned all about grooming a horse, and even how to detect simple diseases, like thrush, and care for them. She could now spot lameness in a horse almost as quickly as Gordon Wright could. And as she worked alongside the grooms, sometimes even mucking out the stalls, Elaine grew certain that this was the life she wanted—to work with horses full time.

Her social life didn't mean much to Elaine at the moment. And she would hate working in an office, although her mother was determined that during the summer, after she had started college, she would study shorthand and typing at Katharine Gibbs. Meanwhile, a daily routine shaped itself, and the weeks and the months slipped by.

Then Gordon Wright announced that he had been invited to form the first Olympic Equestrian Team. Every good rider at the stable wanted to be a part of it. After weeks of grueling rehearsals—with riders from New Jersey, Connecticut, Delaware, and Pennsylvania, as well as New York, competing—a few were chosen to enter the finals. They included Arthur McCashin from New Jersey, William Steinkraus from Connecticut, George Morris, Frank Chapot, and Elaine Moore from New York. Myles was not nearly good enough to join this company—besides he had left to be a freshman at Yale University.

As anyone who has ever ridden knows, Olympic courses are among the most difficult in the world. They are run according to the rules used in international competitions, rather than the American National Horse Show rules. No wings are used. (A wing is a large board enclosing the jump on each side.) Time counts, and it takes all a rider's skill to

Taking jumps with ease and style brought Elaine an offer from Gordon Wright to try out for the first Olympic team

cut corners without throwing his horse off stride.

Eager and excited, Gordon Wright's group piled into two cars and followed the horse vans to Indian Town Gap, Pennsylvania, where they were quartered in former Army barracks. Horses for the finalists, they had been told, were to be supplied by the Army. Meanwhile, they had brought along whatever horses were available to use in the eliminations. Elaine wished Mint Leaf were old enough and schooled enough to use, but the filly was a long way from participating in competition like this.

Gordon Wright assigned to Elaine a little mare named Easy Do—but there was nothing "easy" about her. Standing barely sixteen hands, she had a lot of age on her, almost fifteen years. Also, she was over in the knees, or knee-sprung, which means that she had unsound legs from too much high-jumping. To Elaine, she didn't look as if she'd last the first day. But riders and horses alike were put on rigid training schedules.

"Never start to decide for a horse," Gordon Wright warned his riders, "and then desert him. It's better to do a wrong thing, and be definite about it, than to start to do a right thing and change your mind halfway through."

You had to decide, for instance, which was better —asking a horse for four long strides or letting him take five short ones, whether to cut time with a sharp angle or go in straight and count on a clean jump to make up for the time faults. Every jump had to be analyzed on its own merits and then the course put together, so to speak, in the rider's head.

It wasn't surprising that even top riders took spill after spill. But when you've reached that degree of riding skill, you've learned how to fall so that, unless a horse turns over with you, you land fairly easily.

From eight in the morning until five at night, horses and riders were schooled over jumps as high as six feet, and with five-foot spreads. Then back to the barracks for the weary riders, to shower, change, and drive down to the little town for amusement.

After days of grueling practice, the final team was formed. It rained hard all the night before, and the jumping field was a sea of mud. Worse, the Army horses had not arrived—and gossip now said there would be no Army horses. Knowing that there was no money to buy a proper horse, or even to rent one, Elaine took the field on Easy Do, hoping for the best—perhaps for a miracle.

The fourth fence was the biggest and wickedest of all. There were barrels to tell the horse where to start jumping, a brush, then a post-and-rail fence, then still another brush jump—in all, enough to make a horse spread out almost six feet. With Elaine thinking for her, Easy Do managed to clear the jump. She stood trembling on the other side of it for a moment . . . and then she turned over in a complete somersault.

Elaine lay there in the mud, not caring, for that minute, whether she lived or died. Everyone came running out. "Don't move!" Gordon Wright warned, reaching her first. Gingerly, she felt her bones. All intact—and why not? She knew how to throw herself away from a horse that is going down. But what did it matter? Easy Do would be disqualified.

Elaine had qualified as a rider, but that did her no good without a qualified horse—and no such horse was available. Her Olympic Team hopes were dead.

And, she found, other hopes of hers were about to die, as well.

When Elaine got back to Westchester, a letter was waiting for her. *Myles Fletcher, Yale,* was written in the upper-left-hand corner of the envelope. A letter from Myles was always fun, always welcome. Eagerly, she tore it open. Most likely, he was repeating his invitation to spend a college weekend with him. "Well," Elaine decided, "even if it does fall the same weekend as the big Silver Birch horse show, I'll go. I'm getting too grim about riding. I never do anything else that's fun. I'll accept the invitation!"

But it wasn't an invitation. . . .

This is the toughest letter I have ever had to write. The first line swam off the page at her—into her eyes, into her heart. Then she read on. *We've seen so much of each other—too much—for so long that we've fallen into a habit—and the relationship between two people should be based on something surer than merely habit. It's not fair to either of us. . . .*

Suddenly Elaine crumpled the letter into a ball and flung it away from her. "All summer he's been trying to make up his mind between Marian and me," she thought. "Now, I guess, he's made it up. He's chosen Marian—and all I can do is be a good sport about it. But—but—I'm so tired, so *tired,* of being a good sport!"

Elaine continued to win even though she could only ride on weekends

Chapter Eight

A NEW WAY BACK

One by one, the high-school years slipped by, filled with school work, with occasional dates—boys who, because they didn't measure up to Elaine's ideas of what a man should be, counted for very little—and with, above all, horses and riding.

Then—"Too soon!" Elaine thought—it was time for her to graduate from high school, time to face the question: "What next?" She tried to avoid making the decision, but she knew it had to be made—and she knew her mother would continue to press her to make it.

"You must go to college," Mrs. Moore said, over and over again. "You must have more education—with no more than a high-school diploma, you can't get anywhere."

Elaine had to agree. The trouble was, she didn't

know how she *did* want to spend the rest of her life
—except that it must, somehow, be spent working with
horses. But a groom?

And so—reluctantly, but knowing it was right—
Elaine went off to Bennett Junior College in the fall.

At Bennett, Elaine was the top rider in the school
—which helped make up for the fact that she had
fewer clothes and a smaller allowance than any of
the other girls. As long as you can do one thing really
well—another lesson Elaine was learning—people will
respect you. Summers, during the college years, she
taught riding at a camp; winters, she rode as much,
as often, as she could.

She went on dates with college men and men

*John Moffat lived in Cooperstown, where Elaine was teaching
riding. She met him—and began to dream a brand new dream*

from West Point, but none of the boys she dated had the special qualities for which she searched. More and more, these qualities became clear in her mind: she knew she wanted someone who would share her love of riding, someone who wanted a simple kind of life, preferably in a small town—someone gentle and kind and good, but strong and stable. A man to rely on, someone to share a lifetime with. . . .

On the June day when Elaine graduated from Bennett, her mother and younger sister came up for the ceremonies. Over dinner, Mrs. Moore told Elaine that she had received an offer from Hollywood, an invitation to go out and write for the movies.

"Actually," she explained, "by Hollywood standards it doesn't pay very much, but it's enough. And the climate will be much better for Pamela. The thing is, Elaine—what about you?"

"I don't want to go," Elaine told her. She knew that at once.

Her mother nodded. "I know. It would mean leaving your riding—and I can't imagine you doing that for even so glamorous a place as Hollywood."

"You're right," Elaine agreed. "I'll . . . well, I'll get an apartment in New York, I guess. And study shorthand and typing, the way you've always said I must. And I'll get a job. Something will turn up so I can ride again. Meanwhile, I'll be only a short trip away from the stables, not a whole continent!"

Elaine followed her plan of going to New York, of studying, of getting a job. But one stifling July morning, she awoke with the realization that she hated her new life.

Lying there, she let her eyes wander around the tiny, one-room furnished apartment, the closet-sized kitchenette. The calendar said today was Sunday. To Elaine, it would be just another long stretch of empty hours. And tomorrow? Back to the TV station, to the little steel cubbyhole, to the meaningless secretarial job.

"Unless I do something about it!" Elaine said the words out loud. They seemed to echo in the little room, taunting her.

Tossing back the bed covers, she got up and went to the window to look out at the hot, deserted street. Up in Westchester, the kids she had grown up with would be getting ready for a horse show, or perhaps a trip to the beach. But now, Elaine could manage to get to the stable only once a week—and that wasn't enough, either for her own satisfaction or to keep up with her riding. Gordon Wright had told her that when, a while back, he watched her in the show ring. "If you're going to ride top show horses," he had said, "you've got to get up to the stable at least three times a week. You need that much practice."

But how could she, when she had a full-time

job? She couldn't ask her mother for help. If she wanted to have a riding career she would have to find some other way.

Idly, moving about the confining room, Elaine picked up a book on horsemanship written by a girl she used to ride with. Flipping through it, she saw a chapter on learning how to use spurs properly on a jumping horse.

All at once she was back in the indoor ring at Secor Farms. A horse show was being held, and she was to ride Mint Leaf over fences for the first time. Elaine knew that never in her life would she

Elaine taught riding to pay for her horse's board. Here she demonstrates for some young students how to saddle up

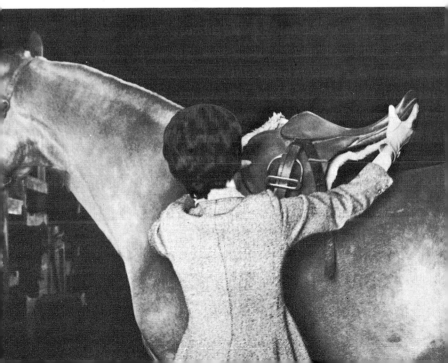

forget that experience. Here she was, winner of the National Horsemanship Championship over jumps, and as she and Mint Leaf sailed over the jumps, the bars came crashing down behind her. Crash, crash, crash—in awful succession, as Mint Leaf reached for one fence, got in too close on another fence, tried to shy on a third.

When the nightmare was mercifully over, Elaine handed the horse to the groom and said, "If Mr. Wright wants me, tell him I've left the country. He'll never let me on Mint Leaf's back again!"

But as she tried to duck out through the rear end of the stable, she found Gordon Wright waiting, a grin as big as a rising sun on his face. In his hand, he held a pair of silver spurs.

"Here you are, Elaine. You just won your spurs."

Elaine could only stare at him. "Won my spurs? Did you see what I just did in there?"

"Of course—you did exactly what I've told you to do. I've always said that I don't care if the horse turns himself inside out—all I'm interested in is seeing that *you* do your job. Then we'll give the horse another school to see that he does his job. So here you are, my girl. You never once changed your style of riding even though every fence in the place came down, even though the mare's still too green."

The distant honk of a taxi horn from the street below brought Elaine back to the reality of the stifling room, the book she held in her hands. Now she knew what she could do! If this girl could write a book on learning how to ride, if Gordon Wright could write one—why couldn't she? Brought up by a writer and with all her own knowledge and teaching experience in riding—why, it was a natural!

She already had the title: *Winning Your Spurs.* All that remained was backbreakingly hard work. Every night Elaine would come home from her job, shower, fix herself a light supper, and sit down at her typewriter. But the effort wasn't wasted. Two weeks after she had typed the last page, a famous publishing company notified Elaine that they would be happy to publish *Winning Your Spurs.*

Joe Louis once said, when asked the secret of his rise to the top in the prize ring, "Hunger makes champions." Elaine had found out how true that was. She knew then—and knew for all time—that anyone can get what she wants if she just wants it hard enough. With a brand-new career, brand-new recognition as author of a book on riding, she was once more on her way back to the world of horses and hunts and horse shows.

An offer came from an exclusive girl's school asking whether Elaine would be interested in coming to Cooperstown, New York, to teach.

On the very day she reported for work, Elaine met John Moffat—and lost her heart.

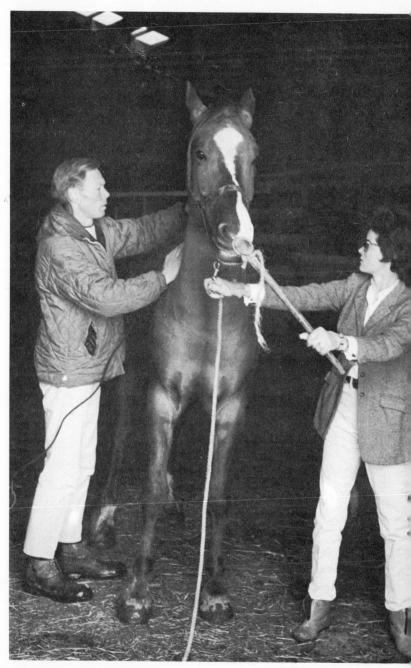
Dorchester Lad, a thoroughbred, was the Moffats' first stud horse

Chapter Nine

CATCHING
UP
WITH LOVE

Ralph Waldo Emerson once wrote, "Never worry about your future, it's all there waiting for you to catch up with it." To Elaine Moore, the words seemed written just for her. She fell in love with the small summer resort town of Cooperstown as promptly and almost as eagerly as she fell in love with the tall, fair-haired young man with the blue eyes and the slow smile who said to her, that first day, "So you're the new riding instructor. You wouldn't like to give me a few lessons, would you?"

"Depends on what kind of lessons," she said fliply, to which John replied, "To tell you the truth, now that I see how pretty you are, I guess I'll take just about anything you have to offer."

From then on, John Moffat's dairy truck was a familiar sight before the school where Elaine taught.

Horses, like people, respond to the moods of those around them. Elaine's mount answers her gaiety with a "horse laugh"

When the day's work was over, Elaine and John would chase one another around the ring on horseback like a pair of kids. And, in a way, Elaine felt like a kid. After so many uncertain, unhappy years, she had finally come into her own.

During the Easter holidays, when Elaine left to spend the week in New York, John surprised her—and even himself—by promptly following her. Like Elaine, John hated the city. After leaving Princeton University, he had taken a job in his father's insurance company. But a year of being desk-bound had convinced him that the city, with its noise, its cooped-up life, was not for him.

With money advanced by his father, John had gone to Cooperstown and bought a small dairy farm that earned him a living and left him plenty of time to ride his favorite horse, Roulette. An easy-going man, marriage was something he had put off, in his mind, for some such advanced age as fifty. Then he had met Elaine . . . and the local girls had sighed and said, "Another eligible bachelor gone."

Elaine's mother was dismayed, at first, to think Elaine really wanted to spend the rest of her life in a small town. "And marry John, and open a riding stable—Elaine, you must be mad! Why, your agent says the publishers can't wait to get another book from you. You could have such a glamorous life in New York, darling."

And Elaine did not mean to hurt her mother when she said gently, "You mean like the glamorous life you've had, mother? I'm sorry, but don't you see, I want to put down roots. I want to feel about Cooperstown the way I felt about Lovell Road when I was a little girl. A place where everybody will know me and our children. A place to live in, to grow old in. Please try to understand—"

But Elaine's mother only said, "All those boys you knew, and you want to marry a—a dairy farmer!"

"He won't be a dairy farmer for long. We'll sell the dairy and pool our money and buy a riding stable, even if it's only big enough for three horses!" Then she clapped a hand to her mouth and laughed. "Good heavens, here I am selling the man's business and planning his whole life for him, and he hasn't even asked me to marry him yet!"

"Don't worry, he will. And you're twenty-one." Her mother gave her, at last, a rueful smile. "So there's nothing much I can do about it, is there?"

Elaine and John were married very quietly that summer, with just a few close friends and members of their immediate families present. There wasn't money for an engagement ring because they had agreed to save every penny they could get their hands on toward the farm they were going to buy when they saw the right place. They went home to a tiny house in Middlefield, the next town.

Cooperstown is a northern New York resort, built on low-lying hills so that the view constantly comes as a surprise. For miles and miles there is the quiet beauty of Otsego Lake, crowded with visitors in the summertime, given over to the ice fishermen through the long, stark winters. For most of the year, the town's single Main Street and the dozen or so stores along it play host only to the town's two thousand inhabitants.

This was the town of which, unknowingly,

Elaine had dreamed for many years. Now her life and her future were in her own hands and she must learn to know this town and love it—as, she hoped, the town would learn to know and accept her.

The little house in Middlefield claimed all the Moffats' time and attention on weekends. John's dairy business kept him busy during the week, and Elaine decided to get a secretarial job at a small local hospital. If their dream of a horse farm were to be realized, they would both have to work hard, to sacrifice personal desires—such as a new car or new rugs for the house—and live by the old New England adage of "make do or do without."

They hadn't planned on having children so soon, and yet Elaine and John were both overwhelmed with joy when first Pamela, whom Elaine named after her younger sister, and then a year later Michael Moffat were born.

"We'd better hurry up and get that horse farm," John said, grinning, when Elaine was pregnant with Michael, and Pam was a golden-haired imp trotting about the house at her heels. "At the rate we're going—two children in two-and-a-half years—we'll be needing it."

But Michael didn't come into the world with the ease with which Pam had announced herself. All through the long, hot summer Elaine was ill. John's business wasn't doing well, and they knew they

After a full day of teaching and stable work, the Moffat family liked to relax by riding together around the farm

must sell it soon while they could still make a profit. They had a small riding stable out in Flye Creek where Elaine gave lessons right up until two weeks before Mike's birth, having given up her job with the arrival of the good weather.

In September Michael was born, and Elaine and John began their search for a farm in earnest. By that time, Elaine had done all the things a young wife and mother does in a small town—she had become a member of the Fireman's Auxiliary, attended the bridge parties at the American Legion headquarters down on Main Street on Wednesday afternoons, joined the small country club, given luncheons and barbecues for all the people who knew John so well and were now learning to know and like Elaine.

"For a New York girl," said one of John's closest friends one day, "you certainly are nice and friendly and down to earth." Hearing that, John told his wife, "You've got it made. Coming from anyone in Cooperstown, that's real praise."

Then the real-estate man called and said, "Elaine, I think I've got your farm." The minute she saw it, Elaine lost her heart to it. There were huge old trees, planted by the grandfather of the elderly man who now lived alone in one room of the fourteen-room house. There was a magnificent view of the surrounding countryside from its hilltop site. There were a hundred acres of pasture and woodland.

Elaine closed her eyes against the place as it was—the sagging timbers, the peeling wallpaper—and saw it as it would be: the barns painted, the pasture land fenced in, the pumps in place, the house remodeled.

"We'll take it," Elaine told the real-estate man, and by the time John's business was disposed of, mortgage details arranged, and the deal closed, it was another spring.

"I'll never move again," Elaine sighed, viewing the vanload of household goods as it headed off toward what would be Marevilles Farm. "This is going to be our home for as long as we live."

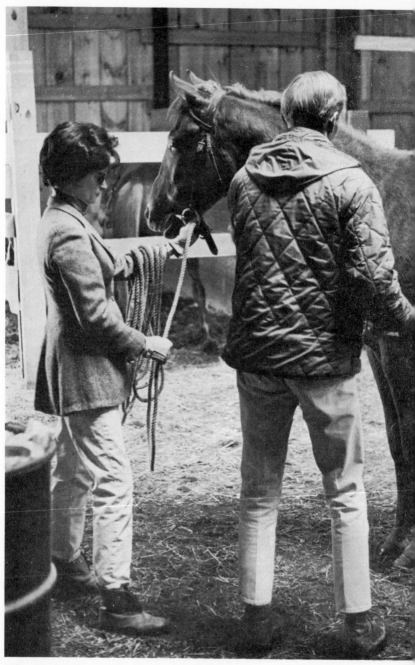

The Moffats faced the future: could they hope to overcome such odds?

Chapter Ten

LETTER
TO A
STRANGER

Elaine didn't know how long she had been standing there, in her hand that picture of herself going over a brush fence at the Sands Point Horse Show. The past had blended with the present and with the future until, bringing her mind back to her own farmhouse living room as she heard John stamp into the kitchen, she almost felt as though she had been reading someone else's story.

"That girl," she found herself thinking, a little proudly, "never had it easy. She had to struggle and struggle—for good horses to ride, for lessons. She even mucked out stalls when she had to and never said, 'I'm licked. I can't go on.' She did go on—and I'll go on. *We'll* go on. We *have* to go on."

"Well," John said, coming in to stand wearily against the side of the door, "it's all over. We haven't even got what we began with. We're absolutely flat busted. We started here with two horses —Mint Leaf and Roulette—and all we have left is Mint Leaf."

He took off his short leather jacket and tossed it on a chair, then stiffly, slowly, lowered himself into it. Tearing out the stalls that had housed the infected horses had been brutally hard work. So had running the tractor to turn over the ground in the lower pasture just before the latest freeze had hit the town.

"It's no use, Elaine," John said, stretching long legs out in front of him, examining the toes of his boots as though he had never seen a boot before, "We're licked. The people who said this would put us out of business were right. We have no money to buy new school horses. If we did get some on credit, we'd never be able to get them broken in time for the summer riding season. The old boarders are going to be afraid to come back until we find some new people who'll have faith in us."

"People aren't going to have faith in us if we feel this way about ourselves, John. We're not licked. We *can't* be licked. If the hack stable is gone for a year, we'll do something else. We'll—we'll start a breeding farm. We'll get Mint Leaf bred, and—"

"With what money?" John interrupted. "Why, it costs as high as a thousand dollars to breed a mare to a halfway decent stud. And then it's a year before she drops her foal—"

"But if we could get a couple of mares already in foal?" Elaine's mind raced on. "John, we're so well known in the horse business. I'm sure if we get in touch with someone—why, someone will help us. I know Gordon Wright will do anything he can."

"Sure, but what can he do? Those people who ride with him aren't going to ship ten-thousand-dollar show horses up here, to a place that's been wiped out by swamp fever."

"No," Elaine agreed, the old picture of herself still in her mind. "But lots of those women keep horses that are too old to show or too lame—like that horse of Mrs. Peterson's. If we fixed up big box stalls suitable for brood mares, and cleaned the place up and all, I'm sure Gordon could talk them into sending a couple of horses up here. Even if we only charged fifty dollars a month, it would be a start, John."

"A start! We made a start, almost seven years ago. No," he said, rising and heading toward the stairs and a hot shower, "you can go on if you like, Elaine, but I've had it. Running around borrowing money again, watching you get half-killed by out-law horses from the west, coaxing people back to ride with us—Pop said that if this thing fell through because of the swamp fever, I could come back to

Mint Leaf, the only horse to remain with the Moffats from the beginning, brings a new entry to the Cooperstown farm

New York and get a job with his insurance company. I could go back to college, nights, and maybe work for a law degree."

"But you'd hate that! You hate New York and office work. We're horse people, John, not office workers. We can't give up. I won't give up!"

"Well, if you find any quick solutions, let me know. As for me, I'm fresh out . . ." He went to the window to look for one last time at the big truck that was carrying away the bodies of the last of their horses. John was not a soft man, not a man who cried. But Elaine knew that when he brushed the back of his hand across his eyes, it was to brush away the mist of tears he couldn't help. Then he climbed the stairs and left her there, staring at the telephone.

That man . . . that man, a year or so ago, who gave a lecture on breeding down in Utica. What was his name? Walsh? Yes, that was it, Johnny Walsh. He had sounded like a man who really loved horses, just as she and John did, and who wasn't in it just for the money. He lived somewhere in Massachusetts. She had written his address on a piece of paper. It was farfetched, she knew, to expect a perfect stranger to come to their assistance. And yet, among horsemen, the bond of their common love of horses, of riding, was sometimes a very strong bond indeed.

Hurrying into the den, she sat down at her desk and riffled through old papers until she found Johnny Walsh's name and address. Then she picked up a pen and began to write.

"My dear Mr. Walsh: Although you don't know me or my husband, I am hoping you will be able to help save us, and our horse business, from going under. Last summer, we were struck by an epidemic of swamp fever . . ." On and on she wrote, ending up with her hope of being able to breed Mint Leaf although they had no money for stud fees.

Could Mr. Walsh help them?

Two days later, Johnny Walsh was calling them from Worcester, Massachusetts. He'd drive up to

Cooperstown and look over their place. He had a fine stud named Dorchester Lad. They could have him for a year if they had the proper facilities for caring for him, as Mr. Walsh had more horses right now than he could handle.

"How wonderful!" Elaine cried excitedly into the phone. "Of course we'll be able to take care of him!"

When Johnny Walsh climbed out of his car at the Moffats' Cooperstown Stables, he knew practically everything there was to know about Elaine Moore Moffat and John Moffat. He knew they had just completed the best season they had ever had when swamp fever—or infectious anemia as it is officially called—struck the small but prospering enterprise.

He knew that Elaine Moore Moffat was regarded as one of the finest and most knowledgeable trainers. He had heard Gordon Wright say, over the long-distance telephone, "I'd back Elaine and John Moffat in anything having to do with horses. If I'd had any idea how serious their situation was, I'd have been up there long ago."

With the Moffats, Johnny Walsh made a long and careful tour of the property: miles and miles of bridle trail, a big outside course for jumping, two rings for schooling, a big, well-fenced corral. And since getting the first phone call from Mr. Walsh,

A desperate telephone call to a complete stranger brought Dorchester Lad to Cooperstown and salvaged a Moffat dream

the Moffats had been busy building the big stalls necessary for a brood mare and her foal and other stalls, well away from the mares, for the studs they hoped to have.

There is hardly any fear that will not retreat in the face of action, and this fear was no exception. From the minute she heard Johnny Walsh's voice at the other end of the telephone, Elaine had been galvanized into activity.

"We've just got to have some stalls ready for him to see," she told John. "I know it's going to be a lot of backbreaking work, but if he likes what he sees, and sends up Dorchester Lad, why, then we can ask Gordon Wright to send up any mares *he'd* like to have bred. Don't you see?"

And so John had bent his back to the new task. At first, he had to go out into the surrounding forest and cut down the trees for the lumber. Then Mr. Kenny, the richest man in town, who bred thoroughbred horses for the race track, came forward with an offer of help. Now, as the word went around that John and Elaine were going into the breeding business, that they had picked themselves up by the bootstraps, determined to carry on, everyone took an interest.

One morning, John and Elaine saw the big Kenny van headed their way. "What do *they* want?"

When the manager climbed down from the van, neither Elaine nor John could believe their ears as he said, "Mr. Kenny heard you folks were building some new stalls for your brood mares and he thought maybe you could use some lumber."

Elaine and John merely stared, speechless. Here were hundreds of feet of beautiful lumber being dumped outside the stable door. Lumber worth hundreds of dollars. And with it, Mr. Kenny's manager mumbled, "Mr. Kenny wishes you folks all the luck in the world—"

The veterinarian from the government office said the same thing, showing up to take down the hated quarantine signs after carefully inspecting the grounds and the buildings.

"You folks sure have got a lot of guts," he told John, shaking his hand. "I wish you the best of luck."

But success, as Elaine and John knew, is never a matter of luck but of hard work. The hired man and John started in each morning as soon as John had completed his job of picking up the school kids and delivering them to their separate destinations. Then, one Saturday, some neighbors came by to stare, to say, "You mean you and Elaine are really going back into business?"

"That's right," said John, hammering a stake into the ground. "In fact, we're practically back in business right now."

Suddenly, a neighbor said, "Here, let me have that hammer, John. I'm pretty good at this sort of thing." Then another man, and another, found a ladder or a hammer or a can of paint. The once-empty, echoing barn became a beehive of activity. The women went back to their homes and returned with coffee and sandwiches. Someone contributed a radio, and an old-fashioned barn-building was under way that left Johnny Walsh amazed and impressed when he saw it.

"This is mighty good lumber," he said, running his hand over a doorsill. "Good, heavy wood. No splinters for a horse to chew at and get heaves. Good, big stalls for the mares," he went on approvingly. "Plenty of pasture land for turning them out to graze when the good weather comes."

He went back to the house to sit down with the Moffats for a good, old-fashioned country dinner of stewed chicken and rice. He admired little Pamela's first blue ribbon and the grinning picture of her on her very own hunter, Star General, which Gordon Wright had sent to her. By the time he was ready to leave, Johnny Walsh had made his decision. The Moffats could have Dorchester Lad for a year, without charge. He would also recommend their farm to any horsemen he knew who needed a place to board their brood mares who were in foal.

"You kids have nothing to worry about," he

One of the many routine problems of running a stable—convincing a horse to travel. It sometimes requires a little coaxing

assured them when he said goodbye to them the next morning. "You've got your health, you've got each other, and you know what you want out of life. The rest is just a matter of time."

Once you start to help yourself, to pick yourself up, it is amazing how many people will rush forward to lend a helping hand. By the time the hills around the Cooperstown Stables were green with spring, it was hard for Elaine to believe that just two months ago she and John had been ready to hang up a "for sale" sign on their property. Their families had helped; Gordon Wright had helped. Three mares too lame to show any more had been shipped up to the Moffats for breeding. There was still almost no money, but the empty stalls were filled. Mint Leaf was in foal. Dorchester Lad stuck his beautiful head out of his stall each morning as though endlessly looking for new worlds to conquer. The snow had begun to melt on the distant mountain tops and each morning, now, Elaine and John wakened to the sound of rushing water, the welcome, long-awaited sound of the spring thaw. Soon they could plant their hay again. Soon it would be horse-show time.

Early one spring morning, as they got breakfast together, Elaine brought up something that had been on her mind for months. "John," she said, "the breeding business is important. Eventually it will be the most important part of our business. But meanwhile, I've got to get back to schooling and training young horses for the show ring. People have to know that they can bring their young horses here and have them schooled and broken and turned into winners. That's fast money. The breeding business is slow money."

Frowning, John set out coffee cups and glanced into the sugar bowl. "Meaning?" he asked slowly.

"Meaning that when the horse-show season opens, I've got to have a winning horse. Not just any horse. After what we've been through, people are going to hesitate about bringing their good horses here. But if they know I can make their horses *win* for them, they'll take a chance. Don't you see?"

"I'm beginning to. But just where are you going to get this top horse?"

Elaine was ready for that. "Remember Ken Worthy's horse, Peppermint Stick?"

"Remember him? How could I ever forget him? Last year, at the New York State Fair, I saw him throw Ken so high I didn't think he'd ever come down. And Ken is a fine rider—"

"That's right. But he's not a horse trainer. I mean, he hasn't spent years and years, as I have, training horses for Olympic courses, for hunter trails, for—oh, just everything. Green horses, sour horses, open horses, hunters! I watched Peppermint Stick last year and I think I can train him."

"Look, little girl," John said quietly, "you're a great rider and a champion and all that, but you're also a wife and mother. And that comes first. How do you think I'd feel if I saw that joker get you down and try to roll on you? You know Ken's offered him for sale for as little as three hundred dollars, with no takers."

"I know. That's why he's just the horse we need." Elaine pushed aside her plate. "Look, you know yourself, if I show up in the ring with a new young horse, everyone is going to say, 'Oh, well, he's probably just a great horse. Sure, Elaine's a wonderful rider, but getting a good horse going well doesn't mean anything.' Whereas everyone around here knows what a killer Peppermint Stick has always been. We've made a beginning toward the breeding stable, John—if we can nail down the training part of it, with half-a-dozen top thoroughbreds coming into the stable this summer—why, we'll have it made, don't you see?"

"I see that you're likely to get yourself killed. And I see nothing about this business worth that."

"That," said his wife, "is a little like telling a champion fighter not to go into the ring again because he might get hurt. I can't live any other way, John. All my life, I've fought to be tops in the riding business. You must let me try once more!"

First place—a symbol of dedication, self-discipline and courage

Chapter Eleven

SCHOOLING AN OUTLAW

"Mean horses, like mean people, are that way because they're scared," Elaine thought. She knew that when someone buys a horse with a really big jump in him, like Peppermint Stick, the temptation to put him over big fences is almost too much to control. But if a young horse with a lot of courage is presented at a fence he can't manage, and if he gets hurt trying to clear it, he will often lose heart.

"It's just like a person," Elaine explained to Pamela one day. "If a rider has a lot of courage and not enough experience to know when to be afraid, and he takes a really bad fall, it's a long time before he'll tackle a fence again. And when he does, the chances are he'll hang back, so that his horse loses courage, too."

That was the big problem Elaine faced with

Peppermint Stick. He was a big horse, almost eighteen hands tall, with a sort of pink-white stripe down his muzzle that had earned him his name. He had his papers, and his breeding was wonderful. He was also a beautiful mover—what is called, in horse circles, "a daisy cutter," which means a horse that travels close to the ground and is an easy mount for his rider to sit to.

The first thing Elaine did after Ken Worthy had reluctantly agreed to let her have the horse for the show season, was to say, "If I win a working hunter championship I can help you get five thousand dollars for him. So you won't be sorry you let me have him." Then she started to examine him.

Very often, a horse who either quits at his fences or stands too far back has ringbone, or navicular disease. The saying in horse circles about such a horse is that "it hurts him more to jump than it does to quit." But Peppermint Stick had absolutely clean legs —probably because so few people could stay on his back long enough to jump him!

"But I've got to warn you, Elaine," Ken said nervously, "this horse's mouth is absolutely dead! The only way to stop him is to run him into a tree or something! I really wish you wouldn't try it. I've known you and John for a long time, and nothing's worth having you get seriously hurt. I tell you, this horse is just plain nuts!"

John Moffat keeps his eye on three pupils. Generally, John teaches the beginners and Elaine the more advanced riders

"Maybe," Elaine said, running a hand down the beautiful wither, "he's just scared. I've been scared lots of times, and it's always made me feel mean. Anyway, Ken, I'll start schooling him on a longe line, over a pole on the ground, and we'll take it from there."

"All right," said Ken reluctantly, while John stood silently by, "but remember, I warned you."

Elaine could not help but feel that all her life, all her training, all her schooling, had mysteriously been leading to this horse, this challenge. The times she had to learn to obey orders . . . the times she had to curb her temper . . . the many times she had to learn that when you train a horse, you're not out

105

to win with him, but out to school him. The first consideration is not the ribbon, but the horse.

Early the next morning, Elaine was in her riding clothes and out in the lower ring. The month was May, the wisteria was in bloom, and the air was sweet and warm with the promise of summer. In the far-off pasture, the brood mares grazed contentedly while Dorchester Lad kept calling to them from his airy, roomy stable as he kicked the sides of his stall, wanting to know why he, too, couldn't go out and join the fun.

Peppermint Stick, bridled and saddled, was put on a longe line. Elaine led him around at a walk, at a trot, at a head-throwing canter. Then she turned him loose on a solid, four-foot fence. He stood a mile back, lunged, caught the fence above his knees and turned over. Struggling to his feet, he stood looking dazed and frightened. As a rule, once a horse has been turned over, it's a long time before he'll turn himself over again. If a horse can be turned over, and so be terrified of losing his footing, the trainer is halfway toward a safe-to-ride horse.

Going up to him very slowly, gathering the longe line as she moved, Elaine lightly stroked the sweating wither. "Whoa, boy," she spoke to him softly, "whoa, now. It's all right. Only, next time," she said with a grin, "maybe you'll look before you leap."

Schooling Peppermint Stick was one of the most

difficult, most grueling tasks Elaine had ever under-
taken. Unlike the countless young horses she had
schooled and broken, she had on her hands a power-
ful, eight-year-old thoroughbred—one who knew all
the ways there were of getting rid of his rider.

Now those years of lessons with Gordon Wright
really stood her in good stead. To cure a bucking
horse, the best thing to do is to turn him out in a
muddy corral. When he really bucks hard, he'll lose
his footing and go down. Again, like turning a horse
over, it teaches him a lesson he'll remember for a
long time without hurting him.

But there is one bad habit of which only a
really competent rider can cure a horse, and that is
rearing. Gordon Wright taught all his top riders
how to do this ticklish job, and Elaine had a chance
to try it out on Peppermint Stick before he'd been
with her a week. Quitting before a fence, he reared
straight up in the air, and seemed to hang there
for a minute. Tightening her fingers on the right
rein, sitting very still, Elaine slowly but surely brought
him over to one side so that he lost his balance.
Then, her fingers steadily tightening on the reins,
she increased the pressure until the horse suddenly
began to struggle to regain his balance, lost it, and
turned over backward. Using the skill learned dozens
of times with young horses, Elaine slipped out of
the saddle on one side, using her knee to keep Pep-

permint Stick on the ground, where he threshed about helplessly. Then, moving away, she let him jump to his feet, his eyes rolling in terror.

"I'm sorry," she told him, brushing the mud off her breeches, "but it's your life or mine, Peppermint Stick—you and I are going to go for broke."

Day after day, in addition to exercising the mares, Elaine spent two, three, four hours on Peppermint Stick. Again and again she was thrown, while John tried not to say the words he wanted to say, "For Pete's sake, honey, give up!"

Then, at last—just as confidence is finally built in a rider by never asking the rider to do more than he is able to do—Peppermint Stick began to

Elaine demonstrates to her pupils the correct method of removing a saddle. Stirrups must be thrown over the seat

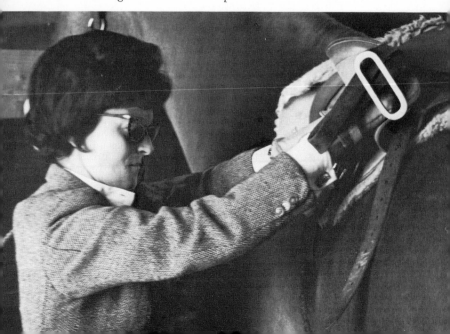

gain confidence. Elaine kept the jumps low, never more than three feet high. What she wanted was pace and control. The jump, she knew, was there.

By June, he was ready to show. Elaine could now circle him, head toward a course of jumps, and know that marvelous feeling that comes to a rider who has a horse under complete control. He responded beautifully to the aids of hands and legs. The "dead" mouth was no longer dead when no one hung onto it like grim death, and the bit was changed every few days so that pressure was always applied in a different place. John invited Ken to come over and watch Elaine's "little miracle." Ken said, "I never thought that anyone, even you, could get that horse to go like that, Elaine. I knew you were good. But you're terrific."

"So is Peppermint Stick," Elaine said, giving the horse a fond and rewarding pat. "He just had to know there was nothing to be afraid of. Now, we'll take him down to that big three-day show at Silver Birch and let him show those high-priced horses what a *real* working hunter is like!" And, to John, "If we win the working-hunter championship at Silver Birch, with a horse everyone says is an outlaw, we've really got it made!"

"Well," said John, "let's hope so, Elaine. But don't—well, feel too bad if Peppermint Stick doesn't make it."

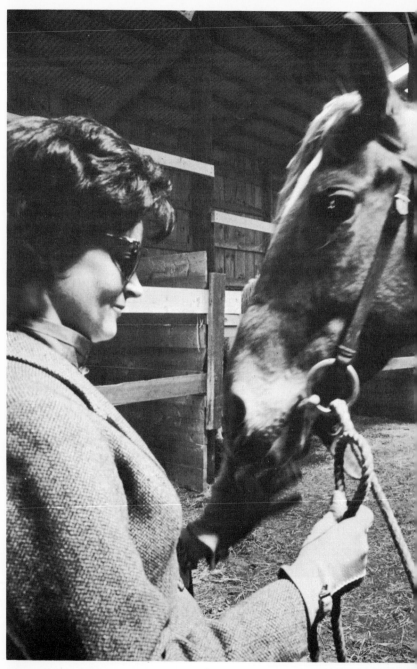

Running a stable means never-ending work, including daily currying

Chapter Twelve

BACK TO THE BIG TIME

There's nothing like the "big time," and the horse-show world is no exception to this rule. Knowing that you're going after the big money, the big prizes, brings with it a quality of excitement all its own. John and Elaine both felt it as their old gray car swung into the driveway of the Silver Birch Riding Club.

For Elaine, it was a return to the scene of one of her greatest horse-show triumphs. Here she had won her first big class with the first horse she had ever carried through from longeline to finished hunter-jumper. Memories came flooding back, tripping over one another. Hunter championships, open-jumping championships, and the many times she had shown young horses, green horses, and was lucky to come away from the ring with no more than a mild spill!

"Well," John said, with a smile, "old home week, eh?"

"Yes," Elaine answered, looking about her at the long, low white buildings of the stables, the Colonial buildings of the private club rooms, the polo field, the horsemanship ring, the outside course.

Then their groom came over to tell them the van, a gift to the Moffats from Gordon Wright last year, was out in back and did they want him to unload Peppermint Stick?

"We'll do it," John told him. "Peppermint Stick never vans well. If he's nervous and edgy, we'll want to calm him down."

But to their surprise, when John led the big black horse down the ramp, he was as quiet as he had come to be in his stall back home. When a horse has finally learned that he has nothing to fear, he is seldom mean. Peppermint Stick, in his day, had known plenty of brutality from frightened grooms who feared to get within reach of his heels!

Young Pamela, who was coming to the show later in the day, along with three of Elaine's horsemanship pupils, had climbed on a stepladder the night before to help her father braid Peppermint Stick's mane and tail.

"Gosh, Daddy," she had said admiringly, "now that he's so nice and fat and all, Peppermint Stick really *looks* like a thoroughbred. I'll bet Mommy

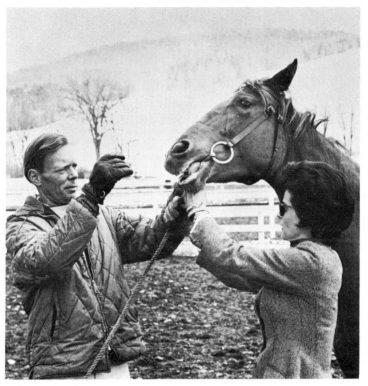

John and Elaine work together to put a bridle on a young horse. The Moffats school and break all their own horses

will win just about every class she takes him in!"

"I don't know, darling," her mother had cautioned. "We're going to be up against some really top horses. And Gordon will be down there, and some of the big Connecticut stables like Fairfield, to say nothing of New Jersey and Virginia. But whether he wins or not, if people can see him put-

113

ting in one good round after another, they'll know the Cooperstown Stables can really school an outlaw horse."

After seeing that Peppermint Stick was bedded down with plenty of hay and water, Elaine and John drifted back out into the bright, hot June sunlight to see who else had arrived this early in the morning. One by one, Elaine spotted familiar vans —Secor Farms Riding Stables, Fairfield Hunt Club, Westbury Stables. Then Gordon Wright himself loomed up beside them, as wide-shouldered and self-confident as ever as he shook hands and asked Elaine how the stable was coming along.

"Much better," she could assure him, "thanks to you and Johnny Walsh. That really was good of you, Gordon, to get those friends of yours to send up their brood mares. It's a start toward a whole new side of the horse business."

"When people start to help themselves," Gordon said, "especially when they've had a real rough time, as you and John had last winter, why, I think everyone's willing to give them a leg up. I'd back you kids in anything, as I told Johnny Walsh. What kind of horse have you got entered here, Elaine?"

She filled him in briefly on Peppermint Stick's background and he nodded as he listened. "I'll pass the words around to a few people with plenty of money, the kind who can put a stable on the map.

For a young horse that has never worn a bridle, Elaine uses a longe-line so that he will get used to the feel of a bit

They've all got young horses they bought at Saratoga. If your horse goes good, they might ship a few young horses up for you to work on this summer." Then he nodded and was off to shepherd his own brood of riders together for a schooling session.

It was almost nine o'clock, and the parking spaces were filled. There was Otis Trowbridge, big and amiable as always, and some of the Olympic Team riders Elaine had known from childhood. Many of the top professionals of the country would be here today, and once they entered the in-gate, all friendship would cease, as Elaine well knew, for the duration of the class. These people, like Elaine herself, were out to win. It was their business to win, and there was no room in the top bracket for sentimentality.

"I almost feel as though I have hayseeds in my hair," Elaine sighed. "How do I look?"

"Beautiful," said John promptly, "as usual."

"That's what I wanted to hear, true or false," she said with a grin, and slipped an arm through his as they wandered over to the stand for hot coffee.

Elaine was made to order for riding clothes, just as she seemed made to order for riding—tall and slim, narrow-hipped, with good long legs that could fit tightly against a horse's side. The yellow breeches had been new last year and saved for just such an occasion as this. A black coat hung in the car for the evening hunter classes, and the classes to be run off on Sunday, such as the Hunter Stake Class. Meanwhile, she wore a white ratcatcher shirt, worn at informal hunts, and a glenplaid coat for the early classes.

"Pam and the other kids will roll in about eleven," she said, checking her watch. "I think I'll get on Star General to give him a warm-up. Why don't you work the other horses for Peggy and Irene?"

It was good to be busy. That way there was no time to be nervous. They would be here all day Saturday and, if they were winning, all day Sunday, putting up at a hotel—which enchanted Pam and Mike, who hadn't stayed at many hotels in their lives. They were sinking a frightening lot of money into this weekend, money mostly borrowed from John's father. If they lost . . . but they mustn't think about losing, or even about winning. They must just think about riding.

The Ring Master appeared in the small outdoor ring, and Otis Trowbridge announced the first class of the day.

"Will the entries for Class Number One, the Lead Line Class, please bring their horses to the outdoor ring . . ."

The Twenty-Second Annual Silver Birch Horse Show had begun.

Elaine watches as a young pupil learns to keep hands and heels down

Chapter Thirteen

CHAMPIONS DON'T CRY

As with a soldier under fire, when Elaine's back was really to the wall, all her nervousness vanished. She knew that she was about to go for broke, and a strange kind of calm settled over her—a kind of calm that freed the mind, even the muscles, for action. In a way, it was somewhat like looking through a telescope. Her range of vision was narrowed, but what she saw was sharpened, magnified, brought into focus.

That's the way it was for Elaine throughout the two-day competition. Little Pamela Moffat won a big class on Star General—suitability of horse to rider—and her grin, as Gordon Wright told her, was bigger than she was. Mike won a horsemanship class for children under seven.

After the first few classes, in which he had been

erratic, Peppermint Stick had settled down and put in one smooth round after another. The hunter classes were being run off in the indoor ring, which seemed to throw him a little at first. The crowds bothered him, the bunting, the swallows that flew tirelessly against the roof, the distracting shouts of young children playing around outside the stable. But once he accustomed himself to the new sights and sounds, he settled down to his job of jumping like an old pro—like a champion.

"That's a good going horse, Elaine," Gordon Wright stopped by to say. "If he takes the championship, I think I know someone who'd pay up to five thousand dollars for him. He's a big man who needs a big, smooth going horse, and that kind is hard to find."

Elaine thought how thrilled Ken Worthy would be to be able to sell his "hot" horse for five thousand dollars.

Now, at four o'clock on a Sunday afternoon, with everyone hot, tired, and edgy, competition between Peppermint Stick and a beautiful chestnut hunter, Any Weather, was so keen that everyone at the show began to speculate as to which one would end with the tri-colored ribbon fastened to his ear. The Working Hunter Stake, the last class of the day, and of the show, would decide it. Out back, and in the aisles of the rear stables, some of the professionals were busy poling their horses almost unmercifully to be sure they'd put in big jumps, as the hunter stake, unlike most hunter classes, is always a fast-riding, big-jumping, flashy class.

"How about it," John asked Elaine nervously, "think we ought to give Peppermint Stick a little rap?"

"Not on your life. He's going smoothly and evenly, and these judges seem to like a real 'hunter-hunter', not an open-jumping hunter. We'll take our chances. We've won three blues, two reds, and a fourth. We can't complain."

Otis Trowbridge called the class to order. "Entries for the Working Hunter Stake, to decide the working-hunter championship, will please bring your horses to the in-gate."

There were sixteen entries in all, with Any Weather and Peppermint Stick tied, so far, for the championship. "Gosh, Mommy," Pamela asked nervously, "aren't you scared?"

"Don't you know it!" said her mother. But as she walked across the ring to take her horse from the groom, she looked as cool and collected as though there was no more at stake than winning a hunter class at a little show in Oneonta. Afterwards, she had to admit to John, "I don't remember a single fence. I don't remember how he went or what I did or anything. It's a complete blackout—and yet Gordon Wright told me I'd never in my life given a horse a smoother ride. It just goes to show what you can do once your reaction on a horse is automatic. Even when you're nervous or scared, you do the right thing."

At last the voice came over the loudspeaker: "We now have the results of Class Twenty-Six for the Working Hunter Championship. First, Peppermint Stick, owned by Mr. Ken Worthy and ridden by Mrs. John Moffat . . ."

Elaine grinned at the roar of cheers that went up from her private gallery of friends, pupils, and family as she proudly led Peppermint Stick into the ring to line up. All that remained was for the judges to examine him for soundness and have him trot out. If he passed those tests, Elaine had won the five-hundred-dollar Working Hunter Stake, the working-hunter championship—and the future of the Cooperstown Stables.

She wasn't even looking at Peppermint Stick as the two judges ran their hands expertly down his legs. Then they began to whisper together. Finally one of them asked the Ring Master to call a veterinarian. Peppermint Stick, he said, had been blistered for the Working Hunter Stake. Blistering a hunter —at least as far as these well-known, horse-loving, Virginia judges were concerned—was to disqualify him.

As the meaning of the call for the vet began

Elaine lines up her class of young pupils for inspection before starting them out on the outside course of low jumps

to sink in, Elaine was stunned, incredulous. A blister! Why, she wouldn't even let John tap the horse with a light bamboo pole. They never blistered horses at the Cooperstown Stables, believing it to be one of the cruelest methods of making a horse jump big and clean.

But the vet was here and the vet, too, was rubbing a hand down the horse's legs, and nodding and agreeing that a blister of iodine had, indeed, been applied. Changes were made on the judges' cards. One of the judges said to Elaine, "I'm sorry, Mrs. Moffat—" but she looked very stern and very disapproving as Otis Trowbridge said, "One minute please. There has been a change in the winning

123

horse. Peppermint Stick has been disqualified. Any Weather is the winner of the class and of the Working Hunter Stake, with Peppermint Stick Second and Reserve."

Elaine just stood there, watching the ribbons being pinned, waiting for her reserve. It was still a good win, but it wasn't fair! Someone had got into Peppermint Stick's stall and slapped that blister on. Peppermint Stick had been the second horse to enter the ring, so whoever did it had plenty of time —almost an hour—between showing the horse and being called back for the pinning of the ribbons.

"It's not fair, it's not fair! Who could hate us enough to want to do a thing like that?"

But from that long ago day at Madison Square Garden, Gordon Wright's voice came back to her, "When you lose, take it. Never be a whiner. It's even worse than being a quitter."

Besides, her children and her pupils were watching her. *They* knew she had never blistered Peppermint Stick, but other people didn't know it. Other people in the horse world, watching the little drama being acted out in the ring of Silver Birch Riding Club, would say, "Well, the Moffats really have their backs to the wall after that swamp-fever business. A five-hundred-dollar stake class—you can't really blame them . . ."

Just the same, people with top horses didn't take

those horses to a stable that would try to cheat by blistering a horse. It looked like the worst thing in the world—bad sportsmanship. But if Elaine protested, she would be breaking one of the first rules she taught every young person who rode with her: "Be a good sport. That's more important than winning. Never argue with the judges, never complain that you didn't get a fair deal. Maybe you'll lose a show now and then, but in the end you'll win—not only ribbons and trophies, but the respect of the judges and the other riders."

So now she had to take it. She had to lead her horse out of the ring, trying to avoid the pitying glances of other riders. She had to hear Pamela say, "But that's not fair, Mommy. You *know* we didn't let anyone blister our horse."

"Of course we didn't, Pamela. But the horse *is* blistered, and when you enter the show ring, darling, win or lose, the decision of the judges is final. Isn't that what I've always told you? Anyway, a Reserve isn't so bad. And now let's go home. I'm suddenly . . . very tired."

And John saw that she was. The strain of months was finally beginning to tell. The grand pretense of saying to the children, "Now don't you worry, everything's going to be all right," of facing creditors, of walking down Main Street aware of those ominous whispers, "This could put the Moffats out of business." The strain of schooling, finally training an outlaw horse, of falling off and climbing back on —all this had taken its toll of Elaine's strength. She was ready to give up.

The strain had brought the young woman at John's side almost to the breaking point, and no words were necessary as he put an arm about her shoulders and let her cry for just a minute, before she pulled herself together and said, "I'm sorry, but I'm just so ... tired ..."

John turned the key in the ignition and started up the motor just as he saw the rather elderly, heavy-set woman who owned Any Weather trying to hurry toward them on tiny feet that seemed much too small for the rest of her. She was waving at them frantically and Elaine said, grimly, "Maybe she wants to congratulate us on losing."

Then the woman was beside the car, panting and out of breath, to say, "Wait a minute! Don't go! I have something to tell you. That blister—I'm sorry, but you see, I've been showing horses all my life, but now it seems I won't be showing them much longer. I'm going blind," the woman said. "I have glaucoma."

Elaine said, "I'm sorry," wondering what this could possibly have to do with her.

"No, no!" Impatiently the woman brushed aside the words of sympathy. "You don't understand. My friend Captain Stanislaus has been helping me for twenty years. He knows the doctor said this is the last time I'll ever be able to see a horse of mine go over a fence. He wanted me to have the championship for this last time. He just didn't understand that no one who loves a horse wants to win unless it's the kind of win to be proud of. I've already told the judges that it was the Captain who went in and slapped a blister on Peppermint Stick. I'm sorry—"

"If numbers eighty-nine and twenty-six are still on the grounds, will they kindly bring their horses to the ring again. Numbers eighty-nine and—"

Elaine, John, Pam, and Mike were out of the car almost before Otis Trowbridge finished his announcement, speeding back to the stable.

"Peppermint Stick," Otis intoned in his singsong announcer's voice, "previously disqualified, has now been fully credited with a winning round. That makes Peppermint Stick the winner of the Open Jumper Stake *and* the Working Hunter Stake. Congratulations, Elaine," her good friend Otis called down from his announcer's cubicle. And Elaine found herself calling back, as though Otis could hear her, "Thanks, Otis. Isn't it great!"

It was once more September. Only a year had gone by since the day when John's beloved Roulette had had to be destroyed.

Now the leaves were turning on the old trees that surrounded their farmhouse. Once more the big stalls were crowded with brood mares and riding horses and studs. Thoroughbred yearlings and two-year-olds poked their handsome heads out of the stalls in the new part of the barn.

Elaine, coming away from the stables after delivering a phone message to John, stopped to wave to small Pam and Mike, perched on the corral fence ... stopped to look around her home—a framework as solid as John's arms around her, solid as the life they were making for their children. She could use the word now, as she hadn't been able to use it before, because this was the real thing. "Made by hand," she thought. "John's hands and mine, and our brains and hearts. Maybe that's the only way you ever make a real one."

And maybe that was something they could teach their children, Elaine thought, remembering how little she herself had been taught, except about riding. When you have a dream you don't sit around hoping for it to come true. You don't look to other people to put it into your arms. Miracles are out. The only way to get your hands on a dream is to know that you have to have it more than anything else in the world. So then you roll up your sleeves and go after it—all by yourself if you must, with someone you love if you're lucky enough.